The Race between Population
and Food Supply in Latin America

The Race between Population and Food Supply in Latin America

T. Lynn Smith

UNIVERSITY OF NEW MEXICO PRESS

Albuquerque

© 1976 by the University of New Mexico Press.
All rights reserved.
Manufactured in the United States of America.
Library of Congress Catalog No. 75-17375
International Standard Book No. 0-8263-0366-8
First Edition

Dedicated

To all those who have taken my courses and seminars dealing with the societies of Latin America

Contents

TABLES

PART I

Introduction

The one brief chapter in Part I is devoted to the nature of the book, its scope, and the method used in the studies on which it is based.

1 | Introduction

This book is the result of sustained efforts to determine the fundamental changes in the institutionalized relationships of man to the land throughout the Latin American countries and to relate these to the recent burgeoning of the populations of those countries. In a way it is the culmination of some forty years of professional effort to understand and pass on to others verified knowledge in a systematized form about the peoples, cultures, social structures and processes as these are found in the twenty independent countries that are grouped together under the designation of Latin America.

All of the studies contained in this volume, those appearing here for the first time in print as well as the ones that first were published elsewhere, are part and parcel of my lifelong endeavors to play a significant role in helping to build a genuine science of society, that is, a scientific discipline that would have a recognized place among the natural sciences as a group along with other specific sciences such as geology, botany, and zoology. My decision to concentrate my professional efforts in the study of Latin American populations and societies was made only a few years after I had decided to do graduate work in sociology and to devote my life to a career of teaching and research in what then was by no means a highly regarded field of study. By that time I already had familiarized myself with many of the essential features of social organization and life in the Rocky Mountains, the great agricultural Midwest, New England, and the Deep South, and I sought the opportunity to study the Spanish-American countries and Brazil as a way in which a genuine comparative method could be used in sociological inquiry.

The comparative method I have attempted to apply denotes procedures whereby a given observer and analyst, using exactly the same frame of reference (i.e., the "sociological spectacles" through which

3

he or she views societal structures and processes) and at approximately the same time, compares and contrasts various aspects of the
population, the sociocultural ecology, and the social morphology,
institutions, processes, problems, and changes in two or more societies. In my own case, the frame of reference used contains important
components, of which the concepts that figure in the treatment of the
"ways of farming" are specific examples, that never would have been
included in this volume or in any other of my writings had I not spent
many months in the rural districts of Brazil and Colombia trying to
take stock of and describe the principal features of life and labor in
those two important countries.

The actual work of gaining the knowledge about Latin American
societies that has resulted in this and my other books, monographs,
and articles about Latin American subjects began in the summer of
1935 when I spent a full month on a reconnaissance survey in Mexico, accompanied by Carle C. Zimmerman of Harvard University.
From that time on my work in and on Latin America has absorbed
a major part of the time I have had at my disposal. In addition to
lengthy assignments in Brazil, Colombia, and some of the other
countries for the U. S. Department of State, the U. S. Department
of Agriculture, the Inter-American Institute of Agricultural
Sciences, the International Labour Office, the Food and Agriculture
Organization, and other agencies, fellowships from the John Simon
Guggenheim Foundation enabled me to spend five summers in the
Andean countries. On one occasion I was also able to visit all twenty
of the countries for the specific purpose of gathering statistical information about their populations.

Other lengthy periods of observation and study came in connection with the months, during our summers, in which I served as
visiting professor at various Latin American universities, including
the University of Brazil, the Universidad de Chile, the Universidad
Nacional de Colombia, the Universidad Nacional Autónima de Méx-
ico (three times), and the Universidad de Zulia. As a matter of fact,
one can have no greater stimulus to accuracy in his facts and the
validity of his interpretations than is presented in a situation in which
he is attempting to teach, in their own languages, young Latin
American professionals about the nature of the structures and processes of their own societies.

But the concern with Latin American matters did not end when
I returned to the United States from each of the assignments that

took me repeatedly into all of the countries from Mexico to Chile and Argentina. For thirty-five years I offered courses and graduate seminars dealing with the Spanish-American countries and Brazil at three major U.S. universities: Louisiana State University, Vanderbilt University, and the University of Florida. In the course of that time I directed the research of over one hundred candidates for the M.A. and the Ph.D. degrees, including many Latin Americans, of whom about fifty selected topics dealing with Latin America as the subjects for their theses and dissertations. Finally, I have endeavored to keep a flow of articles, monographs, and books dealing with Latin American societies coming from the press. It is hoped that the knowledge and experience gained in these ways will enable those who read this book to gain reliable tested information about the important things that are happening to the populations and the systems of agricultural production throughout the Latin American countries.

Because science itself is one species of theoretical knowledge, scientific endeavors perforce are theoretical. Nevertheless, in this and my other writings I have always sought to deal with actual, concrete societies. This is one reason that materials specifically pertaining to Brazil and Colombia figure largely in the contents of this book: these are the countries that I have studied most intensively. It also is the reason that much effort has gone into the preparation of tables, especially concerning population numbers and indexes, in which all twenty of the countries figure.

Finally, it seems in order to indicate the sequence in which the materials are presented. This brief introductory chapter constitutes the whole of Part I of the volume. Part II consists of studies of the race between population and the food supply in two major countries, Brazil and Colombia, respectively. Brazil alone contains well over one-third of the entire population of the twenty countries, and Colombia, as these lines are written, is at the point of passing Argentina and becoming the third most populous country in the group. In Part III the subject is the growth of population specifically, with three chapters treating several aspects of that subject. Part IV, subdivided into three chapters, deals with the major obstacles to increased production of food, feed, and fiber in the Latin American countries. Finally, on the positive side, Part V in its three chapters contains presentations of three specific things that are enabling the production of food to keep pace with and sometimes to outpace the growth of population.

PART II

The Race in Two Major Countries

Brazil and Colombia are the countries in which I have worked most extensively and the ones for which I have the most complete data and most adequate knowledge of the societies. The two chapters in this second part, one for each of these major countries, are attempts to analyze and describe in detail the major features of the race between population and the food supply in the places for which the essential materials are most adequate.

2

The Race between Population and Food Supply in Brazil

Brazil, the second most populous country in the Western Hemisphere, seems to be developing a population policy that is drastically different from the one that has guided its national endeavors for centuries. As I have indicated elsewhere and repeatedly,[1] all through the nineteenth and the first half of the twentieth centuries *"falta de braços,"* literally lack of arms, which is the equivalent of the English "lack of hands," was the nation's theme song. Strenuous efforts were made and large sums of money were expended for the purpose of securing manual workers to man its huge sugar-cane and coffee plantations and other agricultural enterprises. At first this was by the unobstructed importation of African slaves, later (from about 1850 to the abolition of slavery in 1888) by running them through the British blockade. And for about a century from 1860 on it was by subsidizing large contingents of immigrants from Germany, Italy, Japan, and other countries.[2] In the 1970s, however, after Brazil passed (about 1965) the mark at which the population became more urban than rural, and after it also became a member of the select 100-million club (along with China, India, the U.S.S.R., the United States, Japan, and Indonesia), the policy appears to be changing. At least some of Brazil's intellectual leaders appear to be adopting the view that Brazil should cease to worry about getting plenty of people and become more concerned that Brazilians of all colors and classes become a people of plenty. Such a policy is by no means established as yet but the drastic changes in immigration policy, the virtual cessation of immigration, and increased knowledge of birth-control measures and family-planning objectives seem to be generating a distinctly different outlook on uncontrolled increase of population.

9

In this paper attention is focused first on the growth of population in the huge country whose territory extends over fully one-half of the South American continent and contains one-half of all its inhabitants; then attention is directed to the many effective ways in which the production of feed, food, and fiber is being increased even more rapidly than the population is mounting. These are matters that I have analyzed recently in considerable detail in the fourth edition of my book cited above. In this paper I draw heavily on those data. These are supplemented, however, by some of the more salient facts that have become available since that volume went to press, in the flood of information that now appears monthly about the life and labor of the people in that gigantic country.

The Growth of Brazil's Population

Among the half-dozen most populous countries in the world, Brazil is in a class by itself in the rapidity with which its population is growing. The population increase of 2.8 percent per year between 1960 and 1970 is about three times as fast as the growth of population in the U.S.S.R., the United States, and Japan; about double that in China; and substantially higher than the rates in India and Indonesia. In fact, it is keeping pace with the burgeoning of the populations of the remaining half of South America, and the countries that make up the other third of Latin America (Mexico, Cuba, Haiti, Santo Domingo, and five Central American countries). Brazil and the other Latin American countries together make up the great world region in which the growth of population is most rapid.[3] This statement is valid even though there still is some uncertainty relative to the actual number enumerated in Brazil's 1970 census. And it is valid even though reliable estimates of the size and changes in size of Brazil's population are more difficult to make and generally less reliable than those for most other parts of the Western Hemisphere or for European countries because of the lack of nationwide coverage in the registration of births and deaths.

For present purposes some of the most important facts to keep in mind about population trends in Brazil are the following:

1. By 1970 the population of Brazil had risen to about 95 million, up 24 million, or 34 percent, from the 71 million inhabitants enumerated in 1960. In the thirty years since 1940, when the population

was only 42 million and the huge upsurge was just getting under way, the number of Brazilians increased by more than 125 percent.

2. With the rates now prevailing the end of each year finds Brazil with about 3 million more people than she had at her beginning. At the present time Brazil's population is passing the 100-million mark, and she is becoming, after China, India, the U.S.S.R., and the United States, a member of the 100-million club. It is a matter of conjecture as to whether she joins this limited group before Japan and Indonesia, which also are at that important point in their demographic history, but the third rival for the distinction, Pakistan, recently dropped from the race for tragic reasons that are well known to everyone. Brazil quickly will outdistance her rivals, Japan and Indonesia, in population.

3. The birth rate in Brazil is still very high, probably more than 40 per 1,000, although it presumably has begun to fall. If this hypothesis is borne out by developments in the immediate future, Brazil is on the threshold of an all-important demographic transition. A substantial fall in the birth rate of a country provides the thrust for a "shock wave" that eventually is felt in all aspects of life. Very quickly it produces a decrease in the demand for everything needed in the feeding and care of babies and their mothers. A few years later comes the falling off of kindergarten and elementary school enrollments, subsequently in the numbers of young people seeking entrance into the high schools, and a bit later in the sizes of the enrollments in colleges and universities. About eighteen years after a sharp fall in the birth rates gets well under way, the contingents of young men liable for military training begin to decrease, and almost simultaneously the numbers and proportions of young women in the ages in which their fertility is highest commence to fall off. This in turn generates another decrease in the crude birth rate over what otherwise would be the case. And so it goes, until eventually the proportions of those in the older ages, which at first were enlarged by the decreases in the relative importance of the younger age groups, are decreased by the fall in the birth rate that took place sixty-five years earlier.

4. The death rate in Brazil, which has been reduced substantially since 1930, or probably from a level of about 30 or 35 per 1,000 to no more than 15 by 1970, may be cut still further within the next decade. With birth rates of from 40 to 50 per 1,000, and the high degree to which these produce a concentration of population in the

ages from two to twenty-five, in which the age-specific death rates are very low, it is relatively easy for health and sanitary programs to reduce the crude death rate to considerably less than 10 per 1,000. Brazil very shortly may be reporting such encouraging indicators of social well being. However, since life expectancy at birth is the reciprocal of the death rate, so that in a stationary population a death rate of 10 would mean that the average baby born would live to be one hundred years old, neither Brazil nor any other country can long maintain death rates of less than two digits after the birth rate begins to fall substantially.

5. Brazil has moved well into the stage of its existence in which agricultural and pastoral activities have taken second place to industry, trade, commerce, transportation, and other nonagricultural forms of economic endeavor. This change will become more and more pronounced with every year that passes.

In brief, in the vitally important race between population and the means of subsistence, the increase of population in Brazil is a formidable contender. One hundred million people, annually adding about three million more to their number, with a birth rate that is near the maximum and only now beginning to fall, and with a death rate that almost surely will be cut sharply within the next decade, constitute a major feature of the dramatic contest between population and "the food supply" in the world as a whole. With this point in mind let us next direct attention to the second of the contestants, considering first the actual changes taking place and then analyzing briefly some of the principal factors that are producing the remarkable increase in the production of food, feed, and fiber in the Brazilian half continent.

Spectacular Increases in "The Food Supply"

Since 1950 Brazil has taken gigantic strides in the production of the food, feed, and fiber for domestic consumption and for export. On this subject, however, the statistical data, even when they are available at all, are far less satisfactory than those on the population trends. In many cases the figures published are no more than educated guesses, and often they are not even that. Nevertheless the amounts of crops and livestock products secured from the soil are being expanded tremendously, even more rapidly than Brazil's population is growing, so that per capita production and consumption is increasing to some extent. To be specific, from the information available in the various issues of Brazil's *Anuário Estatístico,* one may observe that the index number showing the relative changes in the volume of agricultural products rose substantially from the 100 for 1955, the year used as a base, to 155 for crops and 151 for livestock products for 1968. During this period the population increased by 46 percent. This faster pace of the increase in agricultural products was registered despite the fact that it was greatly slowed by the temporary setback in the production of coffee occasioned by a severe freeze, which lowered the index for this, the most important Brazilian crop, from 239 for 1961 to 102 for 1968. For some of the other major crops the changes between 1961 and 1968 in the indexes of production are as follows: grains, from 124 to 165; roots and tubers, from 122 to 192; truck crops and vegetables, from 142 to 242; beans and other legumes, from 123 to 178; fruits, from 136 to 195; fibers and other crops for industrial purposes, from 141 to 172; and other crops, from 186 to 395. For livestock products, the increases for the same eight-year period are as follows: general, from 121 to 151; cattle, from 120 to 143; hogs, sheep, and goats, from 126 to 165; and poultry and eggs, from 126 to 185.[4]

Most of the activities through which Brazilians presently are increasing tremendously the amounts of products they are getting from the soil, gains that seem certain to be greatly expanded in the years immediately ahead, may be grouped into four large categories. These are (1) the expansion of settlement; (2) the superimposition of farming as such upon the old, traditional, and rudimentary pastoral culture that has prevailed over much of Brazil; (3) great changes in the ways of farming; and (4) the implantation and promotion of new and improved types of farming. The remainder of this chapter is devoted to brief discussions of these four processes.

Expansion of Settlement

Brazil contains larger expanses of unsettled and sparsely populated land, much of it probably as responsive to human efforts as the areas already in use, than any other country in the world. For centuries this virgin territory has been viewed largely as a "land of the future," and settlements have remained hugged closely to its immense coastline. In recent decades this situation has been changing, and the pace is quickening at which the conquest of previously unsettled areas is taking place. This in turn is responsible for much of the nation's greatly increased amounts of food, feed, and fiber.

In the 1950s, along with the migration of about seven million people (one out of every ten enumerated in the census of 1960) from the farms to urban places, settlement was pushed rapidly into many previously unoccupied areas. The most spectacular of these migrations was the movement of hundreds of thousands of people into the northwestern part of the state of Paraná where a tremendous expansion of coffee culture in that highly favored area was taking place. At the same time other tens of thousands of families were occupying virgin lands in the northwestern part of the state of São Paulo and central Goiás to the northwest of the location of Brasília (the new national capital). Thousands of others were pushing into the valley of the Rio Doce in northeastern Minas Gerais, and into the heavily forested area on the edge of the great Amazon rain forest in north-central Maranhão.[5]

During the 1960s these efforts, which may best be described as spontaneous colonization to distinguish them from the planned settlement projects carried on by governmental agencies, increased in volume and tempo. They took place at many, many places along the cutting edge of the immense frontier zones in the south, central, and northeastern parts of the immense country, but the most important of all were in the areas adjacent to and served by the great new road that was cut through the forest and the jungle to connect Brasília with Belém, the great metropolis of the gigantic Amazon region. Into these previously unoccupied territories several million people flocked in the decade between 1960 and 1970. A couple of quotations from Brazilian sources illustrate the importance of this development in relation to the race between population and the food supply.

The first of these is from a report titled *Transamazonian Highways* (pp. 21–23) presented by Brazil's Ministry of Transportation to the VI World Meeting of the International Road Federation, which met in Montreal, Canada, in October 1970:

> Recent examples in the Brazilian economy have emphasized that penetration roads have shown to be the decisive factors for the occupation of vast portions of the Brazilian hinterland,

transforming virgin regions and deserts in[to] populated areas with immediate favorable responses in the economic sector.

One can take the Belém-Brasília Highway as an example. It is only ten years old, is already being paved, and will be completely paved from end to end within four years. The impact of the road is clearly shown in the following table: [The data in this table indicate that between 1960 and 1970 the population of the zone increased from 100,000 to 2,000,000; the number of villages, towns, and cities from 10 to 120; the number of cattle from "negligible" to 5,000,000; farming activities from "subsistence" to "intensive" cultures of corn, beans, rice, and cotton; average daily traffic from "practically nonexistent" to 700 vehicles daily over one section, 350 over another, and 300 over the third; and feeder roads from "inexistent" to rapid expansion, with 2,300 kilometers to date.]

Only ten years have gone. He who had flown before over those desert places of the Central Plateau and that empty Amazonia, would be surprised today with the vitality of the continuous process of occupation and economic exploitation of the lands crossed by the 2,123 kilometers of the Belém-Brasília Highway.

To complement this macroscopic view of the immense zone as a whole, a translation of one perceptive observer's report on happenings in one specific município is offered. This seems especially significant because for centuries the inhabitants of the once sleepy small river town had languished in the desuetude of a little, almost hermetically sealed sociocultural world whose static condition resembled to a considerable degree that of a pendulum held at dead center by the force of gravity.[6] The fact that the area involved is located well within the limits of the Amazonian rain forest makes the development all the more significant. The analyst first describes the enormous increases in the production of rice, manioc, beans, and corn in Maranhão since the late 1950s and then he indicates that:

The tonic that led to this development was the opening of BR-10, Belém-Brasília, at the beginning of the decade. For example, the city of Imperatriz—[in the município] which produces the finest rice in Maranhão—experienced an increase of 67 percent in recent years, and presently is estimated to have

42,000 inhabitants. . . . The opening of new roads is the most
important development. . . . The increase in the production of
babassú and rice is due to the opening of new roads, which
permit the establishment of new colonies, and form new fronts
of agricultural production.[7]

The results of building the Belém-Brasília Highway were convincing to those responsible for Brazil's foreign and domestic policies,
and in 1970 they launched the largest program of road building and
agricultural colonization in the nation's history. The colossal undertaking has as its central feature the construction of a modern highway extending from the Atlantic Coast to the boundary with Peru.
It is designed to link with modern means of land transportation the
heads of navigation on all the southern tributaries of the Amazon
River, and to establish settlements of farmers and stockmen along
both sides of the lengthy new artery and its feeder roads. The results
of this immense undertaking are still to be seen, but the work is being
pursued feverishly and we have every right to expect that during the
1970s this huge effort to settle the Amazon Basin will do much to
enable the increase in Brazil's food supply to exceed that in her
population.[8]

The Superimposition of Agriculture upon the Traditional Pastoral Culture

As the Portuguese colonists established their dominion over the
half of the South American continent presently within the boundaries of Brazil, they devised a system of sugar-cane plantations and
instituted their new creations in the more fertile areas near the coast,
especially in what now are the states of Rio de Janeiro, Bahia,
Pernambuco, and Pará.[9] Over most of their possessions in the New
World, however, the Portuguese colonists merely established what
may be described as the very thin veneer of a rudimentary pastoral
culture over the territory they occupied and claimed. Subsequently
coffee, sugar-cane, and rice plantations, and especially the settlements of small general farmers in the three southern states (Rio
Grande do Sul, Santa Catarina, and Paraná) have spread farming
activities over areas once devoted exclusively to cattle ranching.

Even the modernization of ranching activities involving the improvement of pastures, the production of forage crops, the introduction and spread of the practice of making and feeding silage, the use of corn and other grains for fattening cattle, and so on, is playing an increasingly important role in the spreading use of tillage.

All of these developments are going on so widely throughout Brazil that it would be far beyond the scope of this chapter to give the details about any of them. One careful and perceptive observer and painstaking analyst, Professor Harold M. Clements of the Stephen F. Austin State University in Texas, in his excellent study of the sociological aspects of the mechanization of agriculture in the massive state of Minas Gerais, however, formulated a generalization about the process that deserves the most careful consideration. As one ponders what this well-informed and objective sociologist says, it is well to keep in mind that Minas Gerais shares a long boundary with the highly advanced state of São Paulo, from whence a great many innovations in the fields of agriculture and animal husbandry are being spread to the less-advanced parts of Brazil. The following paragraph is from Clements's valuable monograph.

Undoubtedly the most significant of the complex of factors that account for the variations in the importance of mechanized agriculture, and one closely related to all the others, is a highly important and long-continued trend in Brazil in general and especially in Minas Gerais. It consists of the gradual superimposition of an agricultural economy upon the old traditional pastoral economy of the nation. In such states as Rio Grande do Sul and São Paulo this process already is far advanced, whereas in others such as Goiás and Mato Grosso it is barely beginning. In Minas Gerais it already has made considerable headway, and it continues to progress. As things now stand, however, the extent to which agriculture has supplanted grazing is an important factor influencing the development—or retarding the process—of mechanization. Where the farmer now has control of the land, the tractor and the implements associated with it are coming into use; but where the huge grazing estates still reign supreme, the use of mechanized equipment is still a thing of the future.[10]

Great Changes in the Ways of Farming

One of the greatest problems I had when in 1939–43 I undertook seriously to understand the life, labor, and social organization of the people of Brazil was to convince myself that the ways in which the rural people of that nation were going about the process of extracting products from the soil actually were as backward or antiquated as they appeared to be. At first it was almost beyond belief that, near the middle of the twentieth century, such immense amounts of human energy and vast extensions of forests and other natural resources were being squandered needlessly for the production of niggardly amounts of rice, corn, beans, manioc, and other staples. In fact it was this Brazilian experience, coupled immediately thereafter with a comparable observation in Colombia, that after more than a decade of intense probing, reading, and cogitation led me to classify all human endeavors to produce crops into six large categories. These are (1) riverbank farming, in which nature's rivers alone are relied upon to produce seedbeds; (2) "fire agriculture," or felling and burning, in which through the expenditure of immense quantities of human energy a "farmer" will spend months chopping down the trees in an acre or two of forest so that when the fallen timber is dry the immense bonfire he can make will create a soft, pliable seedbed into which he can dibble the seeds and thereby produce a few pecks of rice, corn, beans, and so on; (3) hoe culture, in which with an improved digging stick, sometimes supplemented with a crude variety of fertilization, the farmer, now entitled to be called a cultivator, can reduce his annual migrations and produce one crop after another from the same plot of ground; (4) rudimentary plow culture, where the forked branch of a tree, often much like the rude grubbing hoe that preceded it in the scale of cultural development, is converted into a plow by the application of the power of the domesticated ox or water buffalo to the tasks of farming; (5) advanced plow culture, or a highly perfected stage of tillage, wherein the central features of the highly integrated sociocultural system involved are the metal turning plow equipped with a mathematically designed moldboard, drawn by even-gaited horses whose energy is efficiently applied by means of highly perfected harnesses and hitching equipment; and (6) mechanized or motorized farming, of which the central components of the system consist of the tractor and its associated implements, machines, and vehicles.[11] Moreover, as I weighed the evidence gathered by personal observations in all parts of Brazil and made painstaking analyses of available statistical data and of other observers' reports, I became convinced that in the 1950s fully half of all the Brazilians engaged in agriculture were using ways of getting products from the soil that were less effective or more antiquated than those in use by the Egyptians at the dawn of history.[12]

During the 1960s, however, great improvements in the ways of farming were introduced in many parts of Brazil and during the 1970s even greater advances are under way. The tractor and its associated implements, and the mechanized farming it symbolizes, is, of course, the portal through which Brazilian farming finally is entering the twentieth century; and volumes might be written about its role in the great changes in agriculture now under way. No such detailed analysis can be attempted here. It is interesting to note, though, that the authors of an official *Survey of the Brazilian Economy,*[13] written in English and prepared for circulation in the United States, indicate that 1939 was the date when these changes began. At that time they state "inferiority complexes ... in Brazil were replaced by a sense of movement; [and] fire agriculture began to be replaced by the concept of mechanized agriculture."

This modernization of the ways of farming in Brazil is an excellent specimen of the transplantation of sociocultural systems and, as such, deserves the most painstaking study by all social scientists interested in the general process of social change. Therefore, it seems advisable to dwell for a moment on the developments elsewhere that brought to a high degree of perfection the extensive and intricate sociocultural system that for convenience is designated as mechanized farming. The system itself is readily available for transplantation, and fortunately the use of tractors and motor trucks is now so widespread in nonagricultural activities that all of the technical skills needed and the lines of supply for parts are readily available in all parts of Brazil.

The way of farming now being disseminated throughout Brazil was developed directly out of the most advanced stages of advanced plow culture as these had been perfected in the midwestern sections of the United States and the adjacent parts of Canada in the period from about 1910 to 1920. There the tractor, the motor truck, and the automobile quickly replaced the horse as sources of power; the number of plow bottoms, cultivators, harrows, disks, and so on per implement was substantially increased; attachments for performing various tasks (preparation of the seedbed, planting, the insertion of fertilizers, the application of herbicides and pesticides, and the making of furrows) during a single trip over the land were devised and tested; the principles of genetics were applied on a large scale in the production of seeds that would greatly increase the product per acre; the combine for harvesting and threshing grain and the corn picker were perfected, and the equipment for making hay and that needed in the preparation of silage were greatly improved; electricity was brought to the barns and milking sheds to power milking machines, water pumps, grinding machines, and other labor-saving equipment; and gasoline motors became the sources of energy used in the performance of a great many farm tasks. Perhaps the most revolutionary feature of all of these, however, was the attainment of the major objective of the entire search for improved ways of farming, namely, to enable one man, usually the farm operator himself, to perform any and all of the large and complicated processes. Simultaneously, the roads and highways were improved to the extent that even "farm-to-market roads" became "all-weather" arteries of transportation; and hundreds of other advanced features became integral parts of the remarkable mechanized way of farming. By 1950, this superbly effective sociocultural entity was almost universally in use throughout the United States and Canada, widely used in Europe, and readily available for implantation or transplantation in other parts of the world.

In recent years Brazil has become one of the chief beneficiaries of this ultramodern way of farming. Furthermore, unlike the situation in the United States, where in the most densely populated rural districts such as the cotton belt in the South the mechanization of agriculture has been a response to the flight of people from the land about as much as it has been a factor promoting rural-urban migrations, in the immense and sparsely populated pastoral regions of Brazil the introduction of the mechanized way of farming creates a need for many additional workers to assist in the cultivation of the soil. Certainly this metamorphosis in the ways of extracting products from the soil is, and for decades to come will continue to be, a major factor in the increase of food, feed, and fiber in Brazil.

Changes in the Types of Farming

The fourth and last of the factors discussed here that presently are enabling the production of the means of subsistence to outrun the growth of population in Brazil is the substantial changes that are taking place in the type of farming. Type of farming denotes the enterprise or combination of enterprises that make up the economic activities on a given farm. Historically, various types of monoculture on large plantations (sugar cane, coffee, cacao, rice) and the "mono-equivalent" in animal husbandry, the production of rangy beef cattle, have dominated rural economic activities throughout the immense half continent. Perhaps monoculture is the only thing feasible in a plantation system, the sociocultural system that depends upon a rigid regimentation of large numbers of slave or semiservile farm laborers and wherein there is a mere handful of persons in the managerial and supervisory roles. With the inputs of management reduced almost to the vanishing point, in combination with the use of large tracts of land and the lavish use of labor, it probably would have been foolish, from the pure economic standpoint, to complicate the tasks of management and administration by including multiple enterprises in the farm business. Be that as it may, educated Brazilians long have deplored the nation's dependence upon monoculture of one type or another. Furthermore, some time ago I personally became convinced that Brazil (and most of the other Latin American countries as well) would never enjoy the productivity and levels of living to which the people aspired until the crop and livestock enterprises came to be combined effectively in highly symbiotic combinations such as the corn–hog–beef-cattle type of farming (this remarkable system was perfected before 1840, and from then until about 1960 it was responsible for the prosperity of the great midwestern "corn belt" in the United States), the dairy husbandry of Great Lakes area of the United States and Canada, or the combination of dairying and swine husbandry featured in Denmark's remarkable farming activities.[14] Throughout the length and breadth of Brazil, however, I was able to find very few significant attempts to combine the crop and livestock enterprises in given farm businesses. The most important I did discover were among the small general farmers in the "colonial" zones of south Brazil; especially noteworthy among these were those in the hills in the northeast of the state of Rio Grande do Sul where the system of growing and transforming substantial crops of corn into lard and other pork products was the basis for many fairly prosperous farming communities. Indeed, as decade after decade passed in which there was little or no visible evidence of substantial departure from monoculture of one kind or another, I almost abandoned hope that some day I would be able to observe significant improvements in types of farming throughout Brazil.

More recently, however, and especially in the 1960s and 1970s, changes occurred that are producing greatly increased symbiosis among crop and livestock enterprises on the farms in São Paulo, Minas Gerais, Paraná, Rio de Janeiro, and other states in the more densely inhabited parts of Brazil. Some of this represents an integration of swine, beef cattle, and poultry enterprises with the production of forage crops and grains, but by far the most important is the phenomenal rise of the dairy industry. In the latest edition of my *Brazil,* I have devoted a lengthy section (pp. 664–76) to the genesis and spread of this highly symbiotic sociocultural system and to an analysis of some of the principal factors that are responsible for these developments. Suffice it to say here, though, that in the areas near the great cities of São Paulo, Rio de Janeiro, Porto Alegre, Curitiba, and Belo Horizonte, dairy husbandry has become a major type of farming. The change is particularly striking in the area of the once-decadent old coffee zone in southern Minas Gerais, the state of Rio de Janeiro, and parts of the state of São Paulo. Among the factors providing the thrust for the tremendous change are (1) the establishment since the end of World War II of a few colonies of European immigrants, and especially those of the Dutch and of the Mennonites from Russia, who transplanted highly perfected systems of dairy husbandry to locations near the cities of São Paulo and Curitiba; (2) the activities of Brazil's new and tremendously important agricultural extension service (the Associação Brasileira de Crédito e Asisténcia Rural), which combines adult education and supervised farm credit, in the service of the farmers who operate small and medium-sized farms; (3) the promotion of dairying by commercial firms that have mounted huge plants for the confection of chocolate candies and other sweets, for which the highly elastic demand in Brazilian cities is almost unbounded, which need the milk to combine with Brazilian sugar and cacao for the goods (or "goodies") they produce; (4) the tremendous demand for milk and milk products on the part of millions of persons, substantial numbers of whom are immigrants or the children of recent immigrants, who inhabit the cities of what now is a predominantly urban country; and (5) the decision by some of the proprietors of Brazil's great landed estates to establish huge, modern dairies, stocked with purebred dairy cattle that they import from the countries most noted for dairy farming.

Already Brazil, from a position that was invisible in world perspective as late as 1950, has moved to the forefront among the milk-producing countries of the world. Brazil still does not figure among the countries for which data are published in the U.S. Department of Agriculture's *World Agricultural Production and Trade* (July 1970 issue), which lists the leading dairy countries in order as follows: the United States, France, West Germany, the United Kingdom, Italy, Canada, the Netherlands, and Australia. But by 1970 Brazil already outranked Australia in the production of milk, and it is almost certain that by 1972 it exceeded the Netherlands, Canada, and Italy in such production. Moreover, before 1980 Brazil seems certain to replace the United Kingdom as the world's fourth most important producer of milk. In any case the upsurge of dairy husbandry in Brazil is tremendous, the potentialities in this type of farming are almost unlimited, and both in recent years and in the immediate future the growth and spread of the almost new (to Brazil) type of farming is doing much to enable the increase of the food supply to outpace even the very rapid rate with which the population is growing.

In conclusion it seems important to stress that to date the accomplishments in increasing Brazil's production of "the means of subsistence" are relatively modest in comparison with the potential. Much of her territory is still to be brought into the service of mankind. Only a beginning has been made in the modernization of the ways of farming. And the possibilities of more effective types of farming are almost unlimited. One may confidently expect that within the next few decades the four great wonder crops (corn, alfalfa, soybeans, and the grain sorghums) will come to be the mainstays of Brazilian farming, and that the abundant harvests of these will be transformed into milk and milk products, beef, pork and pork products, poultry and eggs. These will be largely for domestic consumption in a rapidly expanding domestic market. In the great drought-stricken, problem-ridden Northeast, for example, through which flow the potentially fructifying waters of the great São Francisco River, in the years ahead immense fields of alfalfa and other forage crops, soybeans and milo sorghum, and corn will be combined with greatly improved breeds of beef and dairy cattle to transform that large area into one of the highly productive parts of Brazil. Elsewhere the modernization of the ways of farming used in rice culture and the combination of this crop in the same farm business with the production of beef cattle, often in rotation with soybeans, will bring prosperity to hundreds of thousands of farm families, and greatly augmented volumes of the necessities of life to millions of city people. Something akin to the combination of dairy husbandry and the production of bacon-type hogs, the basis of Denmark's enviable system of agriculture, may be developed at many places throughout Brazil. And such an enumeration of the possibilities might be extended at great length. It is hoped that enough has been said, however, to establish the thought that as yet the increase of population in Brazil is not pressing hard on the possibilities of expanding the food supply. Brazil is fortunate in that in her immediate future there is every reason to suppose that the production of her farms, plantations, and ranches will rise more rapidly than her population, so that she will have the time in which to develop and put into practice a population policy adapted to the realities of the problem of unchecked population growth.

3

The Race between Population and Food Supply in Colombia

In the 1970s the spotlight of public attention and concern once again is focused upon the speed with which the population of the world is mounting. The threat of severe overpopulation now seriously endangers levels of living in many parts of the earth, and especially those in areas where the planes of living have never been anything but extremely low. It is true that much of the concern has arisen in and has been promoted by thinkers in some of the more highly industrialized nations, whereas the current inordinately high rates at which the population is increasing are found in the less-developed portions of Africa, Asia, and Latin America. It also is true that in some of the more highly developed countries such as Japan, Canada, and the United States the natural increase in the number of the inhabitants is near the point at which a stationary population or "zero population growth" will have been achieved. Nevertheless, there is need for much greater knowledge of population trends, present and potential, and especially of the extent to which these are matched by performances in the production of the means of subsistence; I myself have been endeavoring to help throw additional light upon these fundamental processes and relationships. In Chapter 2 and elsewhere recently I have presented some of the results of these studies of the changes in Brazil,[1] and in this chapter I endeavor to present some of the most salient features of the developments in Colombia.

There are two principal reasons for concentrating upon Colombia at this time. The first of these is the fact that ever since 1943 a major

Prepared for the XXIII International Sociological Congress, Caracas, Venezuela, November 20–25, 1972.

25

part of my own time and attention has been directed to the work of
trying to understand its people and institutions and of identifying the
changes they were undergoing; the second is that Colombia probably
comes nearer to being representative of all eighteen of the Spanish-
American countries than any of the others. Geographically it is
almost midway between the extremes represented by the northwestern part of Mexico and Tierra del Fuego; within its boundaries are
to be found areas ranging from the most frigid zones and temperate
climates to the most humid and also the most arid tropics; its agricultural, mining, and industrial economies constitute a "mix" that includes almost all of the kinds of life and labor found elsewhere in
Spanish America; and its rural-urban patterns are intermediate between the extremes found in Argentina and Uruguay at one end of
the scale and Nicaragua, Paraguay, and Honduras at the other.
Moreover, the fact that Colombia soon will replace Argentina as the
second most populous of the Spanish-American countries and
become the country with the third largest population in Latin America is an additional reason for considering at this time the race
between population and the food supply there.

The Growth of Colombia's Population

It is logical to begin our analysis with an attempt to determine the
rate at which the population of Colombia is growing, the trend in the
recent past, and the prospects for the immediate future. Then we
shall be in a position to consider what is happening in Colombia's
agriculture, that is, to examine the rapidity with which the production of food, feed, and fiber is being increased and the possibilities
of substantial increases in the "means of subsistence" in the years
immediately ahead.

The Recency of the Upsurge of Population

There is little reason for going back beyond 1938 in our examination of the growth of population in Colombia. The census taken that
year is one of the landmarks in the development of reliable demographic data for that country, and indeed for all of Latin America,
and in any case the materials gathered in a census attempted in 1928

never received official approval. The results of censuses taken earlier probably are even less reliable. In 1938, however, the year before my own personal contacts with that interesting country began, Colombia made the first modern enumeration of her inhabitants. In round numbers this count showed a population of about 8,700,000. Her next census, that of 1950, was made as part of the Census of the Americas and by that time, beginning in 1943, I personally had spent lengthy periods of time in Colombia, used almost every conceivable means of transportation to visit practically all of the inhabited parts of the country, and attempted quantitative studies of the patterns of growth and depopulation in the extremely varied and heterogeneous country under consideration.[2]

Even before these studies were undertaken, however, I had been privileged to visit at least once practically all of the Latin American countries, including one four-month swing around South America in 1939; I also had spent one full year of intensive sociological and demographic research in Brazil and had the first edition of my *Brazil: People and Institutions*[3] almost ready for the press. Because it helps give perspective to the fads and fashions in demographic matters, and especially to the gyrations in intellectual concern on this matter in the United States, it seems well to mention some of my experiences as I moved down the west coast and up the east coast of South America. Everywhere I went I was asked by governmental officials, university professors, and reporters if it were true that the United States was faced with a "declining population." To these questions I was able to respond with a considerable degree of assuredness. As early as 1928 through 1930, in the classes and seminars of Professor Pitirim A. Sorokin at the University of Minnesota, I had learned of and studied the works of Dr. Robert R. Kuczynski,[4] and therefore I knew of the population trends and prospects in Europe, Canada, and the United States that then were casting doubts on the line of thought that only recently had been given expression in such books as E. A. Ross's *Standing Room Only*[5] and Edward M. East's *Mankind at the Crossroads.*[6] And during the latter part of the 1930s the comprehensive studies of the National Resources Committee, especially the voluminous *The Problems of a Changing Population,*[7] were required reading in my own courses on population. The fact that William F. Ogburn, Warren S. Thompson, and most of the nation's other leading demographers of the period had hands in the preparation of that report helped produce the mind set that at the time kept my contemporaries and me from recognizing that the tide was changing. In our defense, though, it should be said that with the incomplete birth statistics of those days it was not until after the results of the 1940 census became available that we really had any fairly conclusive evidences of the reversal in the downward trend of the birth rate that took place in the period 1933–35.[8] No doubt also, as I discussed demographic trends and prospects in the United States with my new friends, such as Alberto Arca Parró in Peru, Alejandro Bunge in Argentina, and Arthur Ramos in Brazil, I was unduly influenced by my study of such books as Joseph J. Spengler's *France Faces Depopulation,*[9] which I first read while it was in manuscript form. In any case, throughout my lengthy visit to South America in 1938, I had no reason to show concern about a rapid growth of population in the United States or any of the countries I was visiting. Nor at the time, either in the United States or the countries I visited, did I encounter a single scholar or scientist who was expressing any concern about the rate of population growth in the Western Hemisphere.[10] As a matter of fact, during the entire four months the principal concerns about demographic matters I encountered were those of Alberto Arca Parró, who then was engaged in organizing Peru's first census since 1876, and of Alejandro E. Bunge, who was studying the rise and decline of the white race.[11]

As indicated above, during the 1940s my work on the population of Colombia, Brazil, and other Latin American countries got under way in earnest. Among other things, I published a lengthy treatment of Brazilian demographic matters in *Brazil: People and Institutions,* prepared comparable analyses (that have never been published) of the situation in Colombia, taught a course on demographic analysis at the University of Brazil, and included extensive sections dealing with population matters in Latin America in my *Population Analysis.*[12] As a result of these studies I became convinced that great demographic changes were getting under way in Colombia, Brazil, and the other parts of Latin America, and in 1949 I summarized some of my findings and inductive inferences in a lecture at the University of Miami in Coral Gables, Florida. At that time I indicated that

a great demographic revolution is now underway in Hispanic America. Although this lacks the "newsworthiness" attributed to the frequent unseatings of the "ins" by the "outs," the process to which the name revolution is generally applied in Hispanic America, its implications are of far greater significance. The number of inhabitants, the distribution of the population, and even the basic characteristics of the people themselves are undergoing drastic changes. These are the elements of the demographic revolution to which we turn our attention this afternoon. . . .

Let us commence with an examination of the tremendously significant changes that are taking place in the number of inhabitants. The first fact to establish and keep in mind is that in the twentieth century the vast territory which lies to the south and east of the Rio Grande is the section of the earth's surface in which the growth of population is most rapid. Since 1900 no other great world area has rivaled Hispanic America in the speed with which the members of the human race are increasing. . . . Between 1900 and 1947 the percentage of the earth's inhabitants resident in Hispanic America rose from 2.7 to 6.3.

. . . It also is important to note that the rapid growth of population was characteristic of all parts of Hispanic America. From Mexico, on the north and west, to Chile and Argentina on the south and east, all of the Latin American countries gained population at speeds approximating the very rapid rate of increase for the area as a whole.[13]

Shortly after this lecture was made part of the record, censuses taken in Colombia and the other Latin American countries in the important cooperative venture known as the Census of the Americas demonstrated that the generalizations it contained were by no means ill-founded. In fact, by 1951 Colombia's population had risen to about 11,550,000. This represented an increase of 2,850,000, or more than 2 percent per year, during the period 1938–51, and the indications were that the death rate was being brought rapidly under control. This presaged an even more rapid growth of population in Colombia and the other parts of Latin America after 1951, and this matter was analyzed at some length in the lecture just quoted. Textually the treatment was as follows:

We not only know, with some degree of precision, the rate at which the population of Hispanic America is growing, but we also are able to indicate the factors which are responsible for the changes. Let us consider these briefly. Even a little reflection is sufficient to indicate that only three factors can have a direct bearing upon the number and distribution of any population, namely births, deaths, and migrations. Of these, as a rule, the first two are by far the most important; and in Hispanic America very little of the phenomenal increase of population can be attributed to immigration. Even in countries like Brazil, and Argentina, which have been on the receiving end of the bulk of the immigration to Hispanic America, the birth rate and the death rate are the factors mainly responsible for the changes in the number and distribution of the population. In Brazil no more than 10 per cent of the gain may fairly be attributed to immigration, and the proportion in Argentina can hardly be much higher.

Essentially the demographic revolution in Hispanic America is due to a dramatic change in the death rate without, as yet at least, a change of corresponding magnitude in the birth rate. For centuries the various Latin American countries were characterized by exceedingly high birth rates and death rates. Women gave birth to children with a frequency close to that permitted by the physiological makeup of the human organism and the grim reaper cut them down in frightful proportions, especially during the tender years of life. All during the nineteenth century the birth rate in most Hispanic American countries must have been as high as 40 or 50 per 1000; and the mortality rate must have been almost as great. Infant mortality alone wiped out from 20 to 50 per cent of the babies before they had reached their first birthdays.

Except for a recent and spectacular decline in the rate of reproduction which is taking place in a few of the more urbanized and industrialized parts, the fertility of the population has remained high throughout Hispanic America. The bulk of the territory from the northern boundaries of Mexico to Patagonia is still characterized by birth rates of a magnitude comparable to those which prevailed in the United States when our constitution was adopted. But in the meanwhile medical and sanitary measures based on the germ theory of disease have brought about a sharp and sustained drop in the death rate. As yet the registration of deaths and the population counts are not sufficiently accurate to make it worthwhile to reproduce the reported data, but the fact remains that the death rates in all of the countries have been greatly reduced during the twentieth century. Probably, in most cases, the reduction has been as much as 50 per cent, or from about 40 per 1,000 population to around 20. This tremendous decrease in the death rate without any corresponding change in the birth rate is what is responsible for the current rapid growth of population in the various countries of Hispanic America.[14]

In 1964 Colombia made another, and the most recent, enumeration of her population. At that time there was considerable thought that the years of virtual civil war, the fratricidal *violencia* that had resulted in the slaughter of two or three hundred thousand Colombians, would have considerably curtailed the growth of population. Nevertheless, the 1964 census accounted for a population of 17,-485,000, almost six million more than that enumerated in 1951, and showed an astounding growth of 3.2 percent per year during the intercensal period.[15]

So much for the background and history. A decade has elapsed since Colombia's most recent census was taken, momentous changes have taken place since then, and the problem is, What are the population trends during the 1970s? This calls for some discussion of the nature and reliability of current demographic materials for Colombia.

Nature and Quality of the Data

The information about the growth of population in Colombia during the 1970s leaves a great deal to be desired. As indicated above, the definitive results of fairly adequate censuses of population taken in 1938, 1951, and 1964 are available, but even the latest of these already is more than ten years old. Even less adequate are the nation's vital statistics. What figures in the national and international compilations of data on the number of births and the birth rate are not the results of a system of birth registration at all, but merely the number of baptisms reported by the Roman Catholic church.[16] These numbers and the rates derived from them are gross understatements. Thus the latest figure on the number of births that is reported in the 1972 issue of *América en Cifras* is 622,884 for the year 1968, corresponding to a crude birth rate of 31.4,[17] whereas my own analyses and estimates indicate that in Colombia "the actual birth rate is at least 45, that it probably is about 47 or 48, and that it may be as high as 50 per 1000 population."[18]

Mortality data for Colombia are based on the burial permits issued,[19] and they are probably far more adequate than the official data on births. These produce a crude death rate of 10.0 for 1964, the latest year for which an actual count of the population was made, and one of 8.5 for 1968, the latest one to appear in the publications of the Inter-American Statistical Institute.

Ironically, for the present purpose of determining as accurately as possible the rate of growth of Colombia's population, the last of the three primary factors in population change, international migrations (for which there is not even the pretense of compiling data about the interchanges with neighboring Panama, Venezuela, Ecuador, Peru, and Brazil), is the one for which the information is most conclusive. This is because the volume of immigration and emigration is so small that for present accounting purposes it may be ignored without giving rise to errors of substantial size.

Finally, it should be indicated that not even the published official data on infant mortality rates for Colombia, for which the essential information is published annually, are to be relied upon. As given in the 1971 *Statistical Compendium* compiled by the technicians of the Inter-American Statistical Institute, cited above, the infant mortality rate in Colombia in 1968 was 74.9, meaning that during the latest year for which information presently is available there were 75 deaths of children of less than one year of age for every 1,000 live births in the country. However, as suggested above, the likelihood of the burial of a corpse without an official permit is far less likely than that a child will not be baptised by a priest of the Roman Catholic church. In 1968, when Colombia had a population of about twenty million people, and when the birth rate in that country must have been about 48, the number of live births probably was about 960,000, or more than a third higher than the 623,000 baptisms reported by the Roman Catholic church for the year. Therefore, instead of an infant mortality rate of 75 that is secured using the data on baptisms as a divisor, one of only 65 is obtained if the more realistic estimate of the births actually occurring is employed.

The Rapid Upsurge of Population in the 1970s

For reasons that should be apparent from what has been said about Colombia's demographic materials, any attempt to indicate the salient features of the growth of population in that country during the 1970s must be highly conjectural. Nevertheless it is essential to state as concretely as possible the facts about the principal features of the tremendous upsurge of population now taking place in the fourth most populous (and soon-to-be third most populous) of the Latin American countries. Until a new census provides another base line from which a more precise demographic triangulation may be made, it is unlikely that our knowledge of population trends in Colombia will be any more accurate than the materials presented in the following statements.

1. By 1972 the population of Colombia had risen to about 22,-500,000, up by almost 11,000,000, or nearly double the figure of 11,545,000 enumerated twenty-one years earlier in the census of 1951. During the thirty-four year period 1938–72 the increase was from 8,700,000 to 22,500,000, or a rise of almost 160 percent.

2. By 1970 the rate of population increase in Colombia had risen to a figure well above 3.0 percent per year and the index was still rising. Before the end of the present decade it may reach a rate of well over 3.5 percent, although it hardly can come to exceed 4.0 percent per year. Even so, in 1973 the increase of population in Colombia probably was about 800,000 and that figure seems destined to rise each year in the immediate future.

3. If present rates of increase are maintained, Colombia will replace Argentina as the third most populous of the Latin American countries in 1981, but because the rate in Colombia is still rising, whereas that in Argentina is not, that landmark is likely to be passed no later than 1980.

4. As was indicated in Chapter 2 about Brazil, the birth rate in Colombia is still very high, the most likely conjecture placing it above 45 per 1000 population, although it may be on the verge of a fall. To the present writer at least, it seems likely that by 1980 a fall in the birth rate will be well under way and also that the crude death rate will have ceased to fall. If these hypotheses are borne out by developments in the immediate future, Colombia is on the threshold of an all-important demographic transition. A sharp fall in the birth rate of any country generates a "shock wave" that as time passes is

felt in all aspects of life. At first it brings about a sharp decrease in the demand for all the products needed in the care and feeding of infants and their mothers. Shortly thereafter comes a decline in the matriculation in kindergartens and elementary schools, subsequently in the number of boys and girls seeking entrance to high schools, and a little later in the enrollment in universities. About eighteen years after the birth rate begins to fall abruptly, the contingents of young men liable for military training and service begin to decrease, and almost simultaneously the numbers and proportions of women of the ages in which they are most likely to give birth to children commence to decrease. This in turn, other things being equal, produces another dip in the crude birth rate. And so it goes on until eventually, some sixty-five years after the decline in the birth rate begins, the proportions of those in the older or retirement ages that at first were enlarged by the decreasing importance of those in the younger years are decreased by the fall in the birth rate that took place many decades earlier.

5. The death rate in Colombia, which has been reduced sharply since 1938, probably from a level of about 35 in 1940 to one reported to be 8.5 in 1968, may be cut by a few more points in the years immediately ahead. With a birth rate of 45 or higher still prevailing and the high degree to which this produces a concentration of the population in the ages two to twenty-five, for which the age-specific death rates are very low, it is relatively easy for the application of modern knowledge about health and sanitation to bring the crude death rate down to a figure that is considerably below 10 per 1000. Colombia already is reporting these encouraging indicators of societal well-being. In this connection, however, one should keep in mind that the death rate is the reciprocal of expectation of life at birth so that in a stationary population (one in which over a considerable span of time each year the number of births just equals the number of deaths) a rate of 10 would mean that on the average each baby born would live to be one hundred years old. Therefore neither Colombia nor any other country can long maintain a death rate of less than two digits after a substantial fall in the birth rate gets under way. It is likely that in the immediate future millions of people in the United States are going to be dismayed by the rise in the death rate from 9.4 in 1970 to one of about 12 or 13 that is presaged by the plummeting of the birth rate to record lows early in the 1970s.

6. About 1960 Colombia moved into the stage of its existence in which agricultural and pastoral activities took second place to manufacturing, processing, trade, commerce, transportation, and other nonagricultural kinds of economic activities. This change is becoming more and more pronounced with each year that passes.

From what has been indicated in the foregoing paragraphs it should be evident that in the crucial race between population and the food supply in Colombia, the growth of population is a formidable contender. Well over twenty million people, annually adding another eight hundred thousand to their number, with a very high birth rate that still is to give any substantial evidence of beginning to fall and a death rate that still may be reduced by several points, constitute a major feature in the dramatic contest between population and the food supply in the Americas. We should keep this point in mind as attention next is directed to the second of the contestants, considering first the actual changes that are taking place and then examining the principal factors that are retarding a more rapid increase in the production of food, feed, and fiber but that, if the necessary changes are made, offer prospects for unprecedented amounts of the products needed to feed, clothe, and house Colombia's teeming millions.

Increase in the Production of Food, Feed, and Fiber

In the preceding paragraphs it has been shown that the current upsurge in the population of Colombia is very rapid, that the rate of increase has not yet started to slow down, and that somehow each year in the immediate future almost a million additional Colombians must be fed, clothed, and housed. This is a tremendous challenge to those who own and control the nation's arable and pasture lands, formulate and direct its agricultural policies, contribute their labor and management to its agricultural and pastoral enterprises, and strive for higher levels and standards of living for the people who inhabit a large area richly endowed with natural resources. Largely because of several deeply entrenched sociocultural systems that hamstring many of the most serious and strenuous attempts to increase rapidly the production of Colombia's farms, ranches, and plantations, it is by no means certain that during the 1970s the increase in the "means of subsistence" will exceed that in the population. In this section attention is directed to this part of the subject.

Increases in the "Means of Subsistence"

As indicated above, the data on the growth of population in Colombia leave a great deal to be desired. Even so, they are far more adequate than those on the production of food, feed, and fiber. Materials on the latter, when available at all, are little more than educated guesses and many of them hardly even that. Especially lacking are any realistic appraisals of the amounts of "edibles" obtained and consumed by millions of humble rural families as they forage the areas in which they live for roots, tubers, fruits and berries, tender shoots, nuts, small game, and so on. Not inconsequential are the amounts they are able to glean from fields that have been harvested, or in some cases before they are harvested, in ways that have been customary for generations. Obviously the millions of country people who have flocked into the burgeoning cities and towns are largely deprived of such means of supplementing their diets, but the importance of this factor in the changing volume of consumption probably will never be estimated with any degree of reliability. For the products that do pass through the markets, of course, the published figures are more adequate. Those most widely used are the ones assembled by the technicians of the Food and Agricultural Organization of the United Nations. Before presenting them, however, it seems advisable to say a few words about some of the fragmentary pieces of analysis that appear from time to time.

The most adequate of these that has come to my attention is that by Jesús Humberto Colmenares in a thesis entitled *Análisis de la Producción Agrícola en el Departamento del Valle: Números Indices de Producción Agropecuaria, 1955–62* presented at the Universidad del Valle in 1964, and published in a recent work by a team of Colombian experts, Antonio J. Posada and Jeanne de Posada.[20] This study was done at a time when the work in economics at that university held a position of distinction in Latin America's world of higher education, and it dealt with the part of Colombia in which the shift from a rudimentary pastoral culture to an intensive production of crops was being accomplished with the greatest rapidity, largely through the efforts of the Corporation for the Development of the

Cauca Valley. Briefly, it was found that taking gross agricultural production in the department (a major Colombian administrative subdivision) in 1955 as 100, by 1962 the index had risen to 147, or a gain of 6.7 percent per year during the period involved. Nevertheless, the author of the report took a dim view of the trends and specified that during the same years "the population of the area grew at 4.9 per cent per year," so that "it cannot be said that the increase in production has been satisfactory. . . . If one excludes from the index those products which are not consumed as food staples, the increment . . . reaches only 29.2 per cent for this period [compared with a 46.6 percent total increase in production and a 34.7 percent increase in population], at an annual increment of only 4.3 per cent." To this the Posadas add that "this of course means that serious steps should be taken to foster agricultural development in the area so that it can at least meet the region's needs due to population increase."[21]

The same objection may be raised concerning this interpretation of the data, however, that leads me to omit references to other studies of this type: the area involved in the increase in agricultural production is not the same as that responsible for the growth of the population. Cali, the thriving regional metropolis that is the capital of the *departamento* studied, is the nucleus of a metropolitan community whose periphery extends far beyond the limits of the department of El Valle. It also draws migrants from other areas, especially the department of Cauca, who contribute heavily to the growth of population in the city and *departamento.* For analyses of this type it seems essential to include the entire nation.

If we turn to the materials assembled and presented by the Food and Agricultural Organization, it seems that at the very best the increase in the production of agricultural products as a whole and even of food products alone is barely keeping pace with the growth of population. Thus, according to the basic data as reproduced in the latest publications of the Inter-American Statistical Institute,[22] the index for agricultural production in Colombia, with the figures for 1952 through 1956 as the base or 100, rose from 123 in 1961 to 154 in 1968. The corresponding gains in the production of foods alone was from 119 in 1961 to 150 in 1968. In each case the average increment comes out to be about 3.5 percent per year, or essentially the same rate at which the population was growing. There is little reason to suppose that any very great changes in these respects have taken place since 1968.[23] Therefore, we turn immediately to a consideration of the sociocultural systems that have retarded a fuller use of Colombia's magnificent natural resources, and to some of the ways a few essential modifications could turn these into the means of vastly increasing the means of subsistence in Colombia, as has been happening in neighboring Brazil.[24]

The Roles of Selected Sociocultural Systems

For the simple reasons that many of Colombia's rich natural resources of land and water are being ineffectively used and that many millions of acres of her potentially productive territory are either very sparsely or not at all inhabited, it seems evident that the poor showing of the food supply in its race with the growth of population is to be attributed to certain sociocultural factors. If these can be changed or modified so as to take advantage of what comparative studies show to be the more productive alternatives in use elsewhere, there is every reason to suppose that Colombia, like Brazil, may rather quickly move into a stage of development in which agricultural productivity is greatly enhanced. Then there will be far more abundant supplies of food, feed, and fiber, and this abundance will not only permit a rapid rise in the level of living and some closing of the present big gap between standards and levels of living (i.e., between expectations and actual planes of living) but also will provide large amounts for export purposes.

As a general sociologist I long have considered that there are at least fourteen great sociocultural systems that must be taken into account in any comprehensive analysis of a given society.[25] Five of them, namely the hacienda system (the chief Colombian representative of the system of large landed estates or farms), the land tenure system, the ways of farming, the system of land surveys and titles, and the types of farming are of the utmost direct importance in connection with the present discussion. Because of the limitations of time and space, however, comments about only three of these (the hacienda system, deficient ways of farming, and relatively ineffective types of farming) are given in the following paragraphs. These are treated in the same order as they have been named.

Colombia's traditional hacienda system is certainly responsible for the relatively slow pace with which its food supply has been increased in the 1960s and 1970s. Anyone who would understand, explain, and attempt to correct the painfully slow increase in the volume of farm products in the society we are considering, or in any of the other Spanish-American countries for that matter, must seriously consider the nature and socioeconomic effects of this particular type of large landed estate, for it is the one that has dominated affairs in Colombia for the last four centuries. The starting point in such an analysis is a knowledge that at the time of the discovery of America, Spain definitely was not an agricultural country. Instead, unlike the situation that prevailed in Roman times when Spain was a principal granary of the Empire, it was a country in which pastoral interests reigned supreme. As a result of their pastoral background, in the New World the conquering Spaniards immediately seized the most fertile and best located lands, the floors of the valleys and the plains, and turned them into pastures for their horses and cattle. In many places the Indians had been cultivating these areas for centuries in order to produce the crops of corn, beans, potatoes, and other staples on which they lived. The Indians and the mestizos were forced back into out-of-the-way places and up onto the steep mountainsides in order to get land for the plantings on which their very existence depended.[26] In many parts of Colombia, including the extensive coastal plains along the Caribbean, much of the Indian population was decimated, and the incorporation of their lands into a few extensive and extremely rudimentary cattle haciendas amounted largely to putting large expanses of very fertile land into immense "soil banks," in which they languished for about four hundred years. In some of the more densely populated parts of the high Andes, however, the brusque changes in land-use practices had more disastrous effects. Crops were forced away from the level floors of the valleys and up onto the surrounding hillsides, where tillage soon converted tremendous areas into deeply eroded "badlands" for which restoration seems to be impossible. In the writings, first published a century ago, of Manuel Ancizar, the highly perceptive secretary to the noted Codazzi Commission, one gets abundant description and laments about the process and its effects. Consider, for example, two brief extracts from his invaluable descriptions.

From Bogotá to Zipaquirá it is ten granadian leagues of level road, whose greater part has the same floor . . . upon which the innocent Chibchas lived and worked. They . . . were cultivating palm by palm the entire plain; we have converted it into pastures for fattening livestock, that is to say, we have taken a step backwards, since grazing is the first step in civilization, which is not truly developed except by agriculture.[27]

From Sogamosa to Iza it is something over four leagues of level road, happy and clear through a pretty, green valley occupied by a hacienda called La Compañia . . . the only in the canton in which the large extension of land included in this valley is concentrated in the hands of a single family. . . . La Compañia is simply a pasture for fattening cattle, so that the plantings of the *colonos* which surround it appear like refugees upon the slopes and sides of the surrounding mountains; and the rich plains are occupied by herds of sheep and larger animals, and by troops of mules, an incontestible sign of the infancy of our country is this, with agriculture dislodged from its rightful lands by livestock.[28]

In a relatively short time this process produced an immense concentration in the ownership and control of the land. A favored few families came to possess immense acreages, and very large numbers of people came to own and control very little of it. This maldistribution has persisted, and in recent decades it has become the heart of the issue of agrarian reform, the most controversial issue in Colombia and other parts of Latin America since about 1950. What the proponents are seeking to reform is nothing more nor less than the hacienda system, and the prospects of any very rapid increases in the production of food, feed, and fiber in Colombia in the near future depend largely upon the degree that agrarian reform takes place. Hence it seems essential to indicate briefly the principal features of the hacienda system:

1. The ownership and control of the most desired land is highly concentrated in the hands of the members of a few upper-class families.

2. Almost without exception the large proprietors are absentees, living in palatial homes in the capitals and other major cities.

3. In general, those who are left in charge of the haciendas have very little knowledge of modern agriculture and animal husbandry. Most of them are merely some of the most trusted members of the uneducated *campesino* or rural laboring class. Because of this, on a

large proportion of Colombia's haciendas the inputs of management
are very slight and often they are practically nothing.

4. The combination of the factors of production leaves a great deal
to be desired. Land and labor are used lavishly, operating capital
very sparingly, and, as indicated above, management is applied with
the utmost parsimony.

5. On most of Colombia's haciendas a rudimentary cattle ranching is the sole enterprise, although in recent years the proprietors of
some of them have plunged into the production of such annuals as
rice and cotton. The possibilities at present of transplanting completely a highly perfected mechanized way of farming makes this
entirely feasible on the part of those who own and control the land
and have the necessary capital.

6. Traditionally the status of the multitudes of hacienda workers
whom fate, by the accident of birth, has caused to be enmeshed in
the coils of the system has been of a servile or semiservile type.
Personal relationships between the masters (or the majordomos they
leave in charge) and the workers have been of the order-and-obey
type, that is, precisely those that have given the noun "peonage" to
the English language.

The point to all of this is that the Colombian hacienda, as also is
true of its counterparts in the other Spanish-American countries, is
a major obstacle to the modernization of agriculture and the rapid
increase of food, feed, and fiber. If the means of subsistence are to
be increased at a pace equal to the growth of population, it would
seem that major transformations in the hacienda system must be
made. The increase and strengthening of a system of family-sized
farms would be one of the chief possibilities, and the vast expansion
of plantation systems, with their highly regimented labor forces,
would be another.

Antiquated ways of farming certainly are one of the major hin-
drances to substantial increases in the production of food, feed, and
fiber in Colombia. On the other hand, the modernization of the ways
of getting products from the soil certainly should bring about results
somewhat comparable with those that take place elsewhere. Even
today probably at least one-half of Colombia's farmers go about the
work of preparing the soil, planting, controlling weeds and pests,
taking the harvest, and transporting things on the farms and between
farm and marketplace in ways that are no more effective than those
used by the ancient Babylonians. As in the case of the deficient types

of farming discussed in the next section, the reliance upon grossly ineffective ways of farming greatly obstructs the increase in Colombia's food supply, but it also offers possibilities of rapid improvement by the substitution of modern techniques, implements, and sources of power in the processes of agricultural production.

Challenged by the personal observations made from 1939 on in Colombia, Brazil, and other countries, I developed a classification of mankind's ways of farming into the six large categories previously noted in Chapter 2 in connection with Brazil. Each of these is a large and highly integrated sociocultural system, so that the parts of one are not readily interchangeable with those of another. Moreover, at the local level the system in general use usually is highly charged with the mores and other parts of the prevailing system of values. The people in every area need not pass through each of the six stages of agricultural development represented by these six ways of farming, but it is convenient to discuss them in the same order as the ones they occupy in a scale of agricultural development.[29]

1. *Riverbank planting.* The transition from a gathering or collecting economy to agriculture took place when woman got and applied the idea of saving some of the seeds or tubers of the plants from which she had come to expect generous gifts of nature and depositing them in locations favorable for their growth. Early she discovered that the clean, soft, loamy surfaces left on the banks of a receding stream such as the Magdalena or one of the tributaries of the Orinoco were excellent places for her plantings, and soon she came to depend upon the seasonal rises and falls in the streams to prepare seedbeds for her crops. To plant she merely dropped the seeds and sank them into the receptive earth with the pressure of the ball of her foot; the gathering of the harvest was the only other process involved in the simplest of all the ways of farming. This system is far less important today than it was at the time of the conquest, but some survivals are still to be found on the tributaries of the Amazon and Orinoco rivers.

2. *Felling and burning.* This was a natural outgrowth of the riverbank plantings that preceded it. Women early learned to utilize the soft, pliable patches of soil they found where a fire recently had found plenty of dry fuel. Eventually the ax was used to fell the underbrush and trees in a clearing of substantial size before the fire was applied. This way of preparing the soil for the seed still is used in a few parts

of Colombia, as it is in many parts of Brazil and the Central American countries. As in the case of riverbank plantings, it involves no tillage of any kind. Merely its replacement with more advanced procedures can do much to increase the productivity of land and labor throughout much of the great Amazon Basin, although in the Colombian portion of that immense region the sparsity of population makes this and all other ways of farming of relatively little importance.

One important variant of this way of getting crops from the soil deserves mention here, for it is found chiefly in the Chocó region of Colombia. This is the excessively hot and humid coastal plain just to the south of Panama, where the rainfall is so constant and heavy that fallen trees never get dry enough to burn. The ingenious inhabitants of the area, however, get scant harvests of corn and a few other plants by felling the trees and throwing out some handfuls of seeds amid the fallen trunks and branches. There the seeds sprout, take root, and grow, and before the jungle can restore itself, these enterprising "farmers" are able to secure a few pecks of foodstuffs. Advances here probably will depend upon the introduction and development of tree crops (disease resistant varieties of rubber, cacao, etc.) that can replace the native trees as permanent cover for the land. In the immediate future, though, this large part of Colombia is unlikely to contribute much in the race between population and the food supply.

3. *Hoe culture.* In this rather complex and highly institutionalized system a broad, heavy hand implement is relied upon in all stages of the agricultural cycle from the preparation of the seedbed to the laying by of the crop. It is the most widely used way of farming in Colombia. In the production of potatoes, yams, manioc, and other root crops, which are among the chief staples in the Colombian diet, this ubiquitous tool is also the main aid in taking the harvest. Moreover, this labor-devouring system is very important in the production of coffee, sugar cane, and cotton, which figure heavily in the nation's exports, and it is the dominant way of getting products from the soil in the densely populated sections where hundreds of thousands of humble families of *campesinos* eke out an existence by growing small crops of potatoes, corn, beans, rice, manioc, yams, and the other "subsistence crops." The dominant position of hoe culture on the Colombian rural scene certainly is a major factor in the relatively small return presently secured from the use of the country's rich

supplies of land and labor; its replacement with ways of farming in which animal and mechanical power figure prominently very quickly can increase enormously the production per man-year.

4. *Rudimentary plow culture.* The central features of this system are the antiquated wooden rooting plow, similar to the one used by the ancient Egyptians, the lumbering ox, and the crude oxcart. It competes with hoe culture for the dubious honor of doing most to retard the rapid increase of the food supply in Colombia. It has been very difficult to replace this traditional way of farming with more effective ones, however, probably because those making the attempts have failed to consider the whole sociocultural system involved and have endeavored mainly to replace just one of its parts, usually the plow itself, with a component taken from a more advanced system. Elsewhere in Latin America (southern Brazil, Argentina, Uruguay) where the advanced plow culture way of farming has been success-fully introduced, almost without exception it has been by the immi-gration of groups of farmers who were habituated to the use of metal turning plows, the use of horses as draft animals, and so on, in their homelands. In Colombia there has been very little immigration of European or Japanese farmers and consequently practically no trans-plantation or adoption of the way of farming that enabled the farm-ers of northwestern Europe and much of the United States and Canada to produce record-breaking harvests decade after decade for a century and a half. As is the case with hoe culture, the abandon-ment of reliance upon rudimentary plow culture is a requirement if the increase in the production of food, feed, and fiber is to keep pace with the burgeoning population.

5. *Advanced plow culture.* The way of farming that enabled man-kind to advance far up in the scale of civilization differs from the way of farming just discussed in that its central features are the steel turning plow, mathematically designed, balanced, and equipped with the moldboard, and the use of horses and mules as draft animals. In contrast with the old Egyptian rooting plow and its modern Colom-bian counterpart, the plow involved glides, cuts, and turns the soil, instead of rooting, tearing, and dragging. In its most advanced stage the plow itself is fitted with a seat on which the plowman rides, and in all cases an intricate, well-designed, and finely adjusted set of hitching equipment is involved, ranging all the way from the all-important horse collar to the three- and four-horse eveners. It is the net achievement of many generations of intelligent, observant, and

innovative operators of family-sized farms who spent their waking hours in the search for ways to improve the effectiveness of their own labor and that of their families and neighbors and of the equipment and work stock in which substantial parts of their savings were invested. This advanced plow culture is the sociocultural system that enabled a relatively few agriculturists in such countries as Denmark and Germany, Great Britain and Canada, and the United States to produce the food, feed, and fiber needed by their rapidly mounting populations and burgeoning industries, thereby freeing the bulk of the workers for employment in nonagricultural activities. The record shows that it has proved practically impossible to transplant this way of farming in Colombia, and it is unlikely that it ever will play much of a role there in the race between population and the food supply.

6. *Mechanized or motorized farming.* By about 1930 this system had become the most modern and effective of all the ways of getting products from the soil. In it the tractor and its associated implements, along with the automobile and motor truck, the gasoline engine, and electrically driven machines for milking, grinding feed, powering feed belts, and so on, are the core components. It was perfected in the very same areas and by the same class of farmers who brought advanced plow culture to a high state of development. This mechanized way of farming is the portal through which Colombia's agriculture is entering the twentieth century, and in the years immediately ahead the chances are that its adoption and spread will enable the production of food, feed, and fiber to spurt out ahead in the race with the rapidly growing population. The situation in this respect at present is drastically different from the one that prevailed during the 1940s when some of my own Colombian friends learned through bitter experience that the lone *hacendado* who attempted to replace the wooden plow and oxen with tractors and associated implements quickly ran into financial disaster. Then, the moment that the smallest part was broken or damaged, he himself had to attempt to get replacements out of New York. In addition, there were no experienced mechanics and operators to maintain and man the expensive machines. Since 1945, all of this has been changed. The use of mechanical equipment in construction work and transportation activities has produced ample lines of supply, and young Colombians quickly have mastered the details of operation and maintenance of the machines. In brief, an entire mechanized way of farming is readily available for installation at any place where the necessary

financing may be provided; it is supported by the expansion of
Colombian industry exactly along the lines required to build, maintain, and fuel the mechanized equipment. Before Colombia becomes
the fourth most populous country in the Western Hemisphere (probably before 1980) the mechanization of her agriculture is likely to
contribute enormously to the increase of her food supply.

Types of farming that are relatively ineffective is the third and last
of the sociocultural systems to be discussed in this section and the
final topic in this chapter. As is true of the ways of farming described
in the preceding paragraphs, relatively ineffective or inefficient types
of farming are doing much to keep increases in the food supply from
outdistancing the growth of population. On the other hand, the fact
that the necessary soil, water, and climate are readily available for
the transplantation of tried and tested combinations of crop and
livestock enterprises that have produced continued prosperity for
farmers elsewhere makes it reasonable to suppose that such effective
types of farming would greatly enhance the production of the means
of subsistence in Colombia. One of the most difficult aspects of the
problem, of course, would be the education of the rural workers in
the care and feeding of dairy cattle, the use of forage crops in the
fattening of cattle, the transformation of corn into pork products,
and so forth. However, in recent years the most intricate of these
have readily been grasped and applied by their fellows in the most
densely populated sections of Brazil,[30] and there is no reason to
suppose that the rural masses in Colombia are any less intelligent and
capable. Even more difficult than that may be to persuade those who
control the land and capital in Colombia to make the needed depar-
tures from the rudimentary grazing economy of the hacienda system
to which their hearts and fortunes have been devoted for four centuries. If this could be done, however, very shortly improved types of
farming could contribute to vastly increased production of beef, pork
products, poultry and eggs, milk and cheese, vegetable oils, and most
of the other ingredients of modern well-balanced diets.

As has been indicated in Chapter 2, the specific sociocultural
system designated as a type of farming consists of the enterprise or
combination of enterprises that make up a given farm business.
Moreover, the tried and tested components involved in any given
type of farming, such as coffee culture, the production of sugar cane,
cattle ranching, poultry husbandry, or dairying are intimately inter-
related in a highly symbiotic manner.

There are in all Colombia very few examples of the combination of crop and livestock enterprises in ways that make effective use of that country's rich resources, and most of those that are to be found are of very recent introduction and limited distribution. Two of the most striking deficiencies may be singled out for mention.

One of these is the almost complete lack of dairying, either alone or, as in Denmark, in a highly symbiotic combination of dairying and the production of bacon-type hogs. It is doubtful if there is in the entire world any area of equal size that has been more favored with the natural resources required for this type of farming than the extensive Andean highlands. Moreover, huge teeming cities, including Bogotá, Medellín, and Cali, and dozens of lesser ones, offer great potential markets for tremendous amounts of the products of such agricultural ventures. A few far-sighted Colombians, led in the 1940s and 1950s by Dr. Ciro Molina Garcés of Cali, introduced Holstein and other breeds of dairy cattle, and here and there near Bogotá or one of the other cities modern dairy farms have been installed, often by recent immigrants from Switzerland, Germany, or one of the other countries where dairying is a fundamental part of the economy. But for the most part the use of Colombia's rich natural endowments for such purposes is still a thing of the future.[31]

The failure of the Colombians to adopt or transplant the corn–hog–beef-cattle type of farming on which the prosperity of the great corn belt of the United States depended for over a century (from about 1840 to around 1960) is another striking example of a still-to-be development in their country's agriculture. In this case, it is important to note that all of the components are at hand, for the growing of corn, the farrowing of pigs, and above all the grazing of beef cattle are Colombia's traditional agricultural and pastoral enterprises. All that is lacking is the effective combination of the same. Moreover, this is a development that I personally began trying to persuade Colombians to initiate as early as 1943.[32]

These are only a couple of examples of the slowness in Colombia to devise or transplant types of farming in which there is a set of highly effective uses of by-products from one enterprise in the other enterprises that make up the farm business. But it is hoped the point has been made sufficiently for present purposes. Merely the initiation of better combinations of crop and livestock enterprises, in some critical cases Colombia's traditional ones, can do much to guarantee that in the immediate future the rate of the increase in the food supply can surge ahead of the rapidly mounting population. This can gain time in which population policies designed to reduce the near-maximum birth rate to a level that will avert catastrophy can be agreed upon and put into effect. It also can enable the level of living and the adequacy of the diet of the Colombian people to be greatly improved.

PART III

The Growth of Population

Three chapters are used in Part III to present some of the most important facts about population growth and to consider some essential matters involved in population policy.

4

The Growth of Population in Latin America

The tremendous upsurge of population in the twenty Latin American countries during the third quarter of the twentieth century is a unique phenomenon in the entire history of mankind. It contrasts sharply with the rather moderate increase of population in the same great world region during the first half of the century, and it probably exceeded by a wide margin the rapidity with which the number of inhabitants in Mexico, Central America, the three island republics, and South America will increase between 1975 and the year 2000. No other great world region has ever experienced a comparable growth of population over a twenty-five-year period, and it is highly unlikely that any will ever do so. Moreover, despite the tremendous increase of population, enormous parts of many of the Latin American countries still are practically devoid of inhabitants. Finally, the natural resources of most of the countries are such that even with a continued heavy increase of population the crucial features of the race between population and the food supply will depend more upon what happens with respect to the system of land tenure, changes in the sizes of the land holdings, improvements in the ways of farming, and modifications of other features of the prevailing rural sociocultural ecosystem than on the biological ecosystem or the number of people involved. In this chapter attention is concentrated upon the tremendous increase of population in Latin America between 1950 and 1975; the relation of this to agricultural production and levels and standards of living is left for consideration in other parts of this book.

Improvements in the Quantity and Quality of the Data

Fortunately Latin America as a whole now is one of the great world areas for which demographic data are most complete and accessible. Moreover, they are of fairly good quality. All of this, however, represents a tremendous change from the situation as it was in 1950. Prior to 1940 few of the Latin American countries had paid any particular attention to taking periodic censuses of their populations, and in some of them—including Argentina, Peru, and Uruguay—anything resembling a recent count of the population was entirely lacking. As a result anyone seeking comprehensive and reliable information on the number, distribution, characteristics, and growth of their populations encountered almost insurmountable difficulties. Completely inaccurate estimates filled page after page of the various national and international compendiums in which demographic materials figured, and in general Latin America as a whole had to be reckoned as part of the "demographically dark" parts of the world. As late as 1940 any recent census data were available only for Cuba, El Salvador, Honduras, Mexico, Panama, Chile, Colombia, and Venezuela, although older but still useful materials were to be had for Costa Rica, Guatemala, Nicaragua, and Brazil. In this connection it may be mentioned that when the present writer prepared the text for the first edition of *Brazil: People and Institutions,* he had to rely almost exclusively upon the census of 1920 for the population data used in his analyses. Therefore, it was a distinct advance when in 1940 Brazil, Guatemala, Nicaragua, and Peru took censuses, even though for the most part the data in them did not become available until after the close of the Second World War. Also, in 1947, Argentina, which had made no count of its population since 1914, left the realm of the demographic unknown by taking a comprehensive census of its population. The big breakthrough, however, came with the 1950 Census of the Americas.

This historic undertaking owed its conception and inception largely to the genius and perseverance of the great Peruvian demographer and statesman Alberto Arca Parró. Under his leadership at an Inter-American Demographic Congress held in Mexico City in 1943, a request was prepared for the Inter-American Statistical Institute to take steps to have censuses of population taken in all American countries in 1950. Also under his leadership, in 1947 the Institute held the meetings and planned the enumerations, agreeing that on the census schedules used in all the countries there would be uniform questions to gather information on sex, age, place of birth, naturalization, and literacy of the population. Furthermore, in this joint effort much attention was given to securing comparability in the tabulations of the data. As it turned out, Argentina, having just completed a census, did not make another enumeration in 1950, Peru itself (with Arca Parró in exile) did not participate, and Uruguay failed to carry through with the plans. Otherwise there were modern and reasonably comparable censuses taken in all of the Latin American countries, and as the materials from them became available the area as a whole became one of the large parts of the world for which the data were most adequate. Fortunately, most of the countries have continued with censuses periodically since 1950. Data from the two most recent of these censuses in each country are assembled in Table 1.

Rates of Growth

Although the dates at which the latest censuses were taken and the length of the intercensal periods vary greatly from country to country in Latin America, careful study of the data given in Table 1 is the first step in gaining an understanding of the rates of growth of population in the region under consideration. Especially important are the very high rates registered since 1960 in Venezuela, Mexico, Colombia, and Brazil, four countries that alone contain almost two-thirds of the population of Latin America. At the other end of the scale, it is well to remember that even the "low" rates of increase of population in Argentina and Chile presently are several times as high as that in the United States (about 0.6 percent per annum).

In order to get greater comparability of the data, Table 2 was prepared. It shows the present writer's estimates of the populations of the various countries in 1950 and again for 1975, along with the absolute and relative increases for the twenty-five-year period. For the most part the figures for 1950 are just slight adjustments of the census counts made that year, and those for 1975 are based upon the most recent census enumerations and the available materials on current rates of natural increase. They also have been checked care-

TABLE 1

Growth of Population in the Latin American Countries during the
Most Recent Intercensal Period

Country	Intercensal Period	Population (000s)		Increase during Period		Annual Rate of Growth
		At Beginning of Period	At End of Period	Number (000s)	Percent	
North America						
Costa Rica	1963–1973	1,336	1,761	425	31.8	2.7
Cuba	1953–1970	5,829	8,553	2,724	46.7	2.0
Dominican Republic	1960–1970	3,047	4,006	959	31.5	2.7
El Salvador	1961–1971	2,511	3,549	1,038	41.3	3.7
Guatemala	1964–1973	4,285	5,212	927	21.6	2.2
Haiti	1950–1971	3,097	4,315	1,218	39.3	1.6
Honduras	1950–1961	1,369	1,885	516	37.7	3.0
Mexico	1960–1970	34,923	48,225	13,302	38.1	3.4
Nicaragua	1963–1971	1,536	1,895	359	23.4	2.6
Panama	1960–1970	1,076	1,428	352	32.8	3.0
South America						
Argentina	1960–1970	20,009	22,364	3,255	16.3	1.4
Bolivia	1900–1950	1,556	2,704	1,148	73.8	1.0
Brazil	1960–1970	70,967	94,509	23,542	33.2	2.9
Chile	1960–1970	7,374	8,853	1,479	20.1	1.8
Colombia	1964–1973	17,482	23,200*	5,718*	32.7*	3.1*
Ecuador	1950–1962	3,203	4,476	1,273	39.8	2.8
Paraguay	1962–1972	1,817	2,329	512	28.2	2.5
Peru	1961–1972	10,365	13,568	3,203	30.9	2.5
Uruguay	1963	—	2,596	—	—	—
Venezuela	1961–1971	7,524	10,722	3,198	42.5	3.8

SOURCE: Compiled and computed from the data given in the official census reports of
the various nations and "Situación Demográfica," *América en Cifras: 1974* (Washington:
Organization of American States, 1974).
* Estimate

fully with the estimates prepared by the Inter-American Statistical
Institute. It is doubtful that any more accurate inventories can be
prepared at the present time.

Many of the more important questions relative to the recent
growth of population in Latin America can be answered by an examination of the materials given in Table 2. For the twenty countries
taken together, the doubling of the population between 1950 and
1975 is equivalent to an annual increase of approximately 2.8 percent. However, the variations among the countries are tremendous,
with Venezuela and Costa Rica standing out as the ones in which the

TABLE 2
Growth of Population in Latin America, 1950 to 1975

Country	Population (000s)		Increase, 1950 to 1975	
	1950	*1975*	*Number (000s)*	*Percent*
North America	45,500	94,200	48,700	107
Costa Rica	800	2,000	1,200	150
Cuba	5,500	9,200	3,700	67
Dominican Republic	2,100	4,600	2,500	119
El Salvador	1,900	4,000	2,100	111
Guatemala	2,800	5,500	2,700	96
Haiti	3,100	5,000	1,900	51
Honduras	1,400	2,900	1,500	107
Mexico	26,000	57,000	31,000	119
Nicaragua	1,100	2,300	1,200	109
Panama	800	1,700	900	113
South America	108,800	212,500	103,700	95
Argentina	17,200	25,000	7,800	45
Bolivia	2,700	5,000	2,300	85
Brazil	52,000	108,000	56,000	108
Chile	5,800	10,000	4,200	72
Colombia	11,000	24,200	13,200	120
Ecuador	3,200	7,000	3,800	119
Paraguay	1,300	2,700	1,400	108
Peru	8,500	15,000	6,500	76
Uruguay	2,100	3,100	1,000	48
Venezuela	5,000	12,500	7,500	150
Latin America	154,300	306,700	152,400	99

SOURCE: All of the figures given in this table are the present writer's estimates based upon the figures given in the official census reports of the various countries. They have been checked with the data given in the Inter-American Statistical Institute's *América en Cifras: 1974* (Washington, D.C.: Organization of the American States, 1974) and also with the materials in the U.S. Bureau of the Census, *World Population: 1973. Recent Demographic Estimates for the Countries and Regions of the World* (Washington, D.C.: U.S. Government Printing Office, 1974). The figures for 1950 are essentially the same as those published earlier in T. Lynn Smith, *Latin American Population Studies* (Gainesville: University of Florida Press, 1961), chapter 1, where an evaluation of the sources and explanations of procedures also are given.

rates are highest of all and Argentina, Uruguay, and Haiti being those in which the burgeoning of the population is least pronounced. The ten countries in South America have a significantly lower rate than the ten in North America, due largely to Argentina, with its relatively slow growth of population, and Mexico, with its rapid increase of population, respectively.

On the absolute basis, more than one-third of the entire increase in the number of inhabitants in the Latin American countries during the third quarter of the twentieth century was due to the tremendous upsurge of Brazil's population, although the increase in Mexico also was very large and those in Colombia and Venezuela substantial. At mid century, the population of Latin America was divided into three approximately equal parts, namely that of Brazil, that of the remainder of South America, and that of the ten countries in the area including Panama, Central America, Mexico, and the three island republics. By 1975, however, because of the tremendous increase in the number of Brazilians, their homeland contained substantially more than one-third of all Latin Americans.

Heretofore, because obviously the rate of population increase has been near the upper limit of the human potential, there has been little point to efforts seeking to determine whether the birth rate or the rate of natural increase was tending to decline. Even at present our attempts to determine variations in the rates of population growth from decade to decade following 1940 yield very little of importance, except to cast doubt on many of the figures for earlier years, especially all those in which estimates of one kind or another are involved. The huge upsurges in population between 1950 and 1975, as depicted in Table 2, probably are fairly reliable, or at least there is little basis for doubting that the tremendous increases of population actually took place. But except for the probable falling off in very recent years of the rates of growth in Brazil and Colombia, as indicated in Chapters 2 and 3, we are not at all certain that the slowing down of the rates has been very widespread in Brazil and Spanish America taken as a whole. Very high rates are likely to persist in all of the countries through 1990 and probably into the next century as well.

Primary Factors in the Growth of Population

The statement just made grows out of what we have been able to learn from a study of the three factors (migrations, births, and deaths) that alone can affect directly the changes in the number and distribution of any population. In this section we present a few of the more salient facts about these.

Immigration and emigration. In contrast with what once was the case, particularly in Brazil and Argentina and also in Venezuela in the years immediately following the close of the Second World War, migrations from overseas have played inconsequential parts in the growth of population in the Latin American countries in recent decades. As far as their influence upon the rates of population growth is concerned, they can practically be ignored. On the other hand, although reliable data on the subject are practically lacking, emigration from some of the countries, especially to the United States, has become of a magnitude to be reckoned with. The most obvious of these emigrations are the flight of several hundred thousand people from Cuba during the 1960s and 1970s, most to the United States, and the tremendous illegal movement of Mexicans and others across the United States–Mexico border. Some of the movement of Mexicans is offset by a return movement, for it ebbs and flows with the seasons. Early in the spring of each year many Mexican workers return to the places where they worked the previous year, the farms and ranches on which they remain until the bitter cold of the winter causes them to return to the balmy climate of their homeland until the next spring. A tremendous migration of Puerto Ricans to New York City and other parts of the mainland does not figure in our considerations, since they are citizens of the United States. However, it should be pointed out that New York City has more residents who are citizens of the Dominican Republic than any other city in the world with the single exception of Santo Domingo, the capital of the island republic, itself. Most of these are persons who have entered the United States illegally, and the movement continues. Nightly small boats carry hundreds of persons from the Dominican Republic across the narrow strait that separates it from Puerto Rico. In Puerto Rico they are almost indistinguishable from the Puerto Ricans themselves, and thousands figure each year in the migration of "Puerto Ricans" to the mainland. Even in these three countries, however, Cuba, Mexico, and the Dominican Republic, the present numbers of inhabitants and the rates of growth of the populations probably are not greatly different than would be the case were there no such emigrations.

Finally, there is the matter of the greatest unknown of all, namely the magnitude of the migrations between the Latin American countries themselves. Historically, some of these movements of people have been of considerable importance in the growth of population in a few pairs of countries such as Haiti and Cuba, Haiti and the Dominican Republic, El Salvador and Honduras, Nicaragua and Costa Rica, Ecuador and Colombia, Bolivia and Argentina, Chile

and Argentina, Paraguay and Argentina, and Paraguay and Brazil.[1]
In the 1970s, however, some of these no longer are of any importance, so that the growth of population in Haiti is not reduced by the
movement of Haitians to Cuba and that in El Salvador is not held
down by the emigration across the boundary into Honduras. Nevertheless, the migration of Haitians to the Dominican Republic is still
a factor to be considered in the study of the growth of population
in those two countries, as are the migration of Nicaraguans to Costa
Rica, the movement of Bolivians to Argentina, and the flow of
Paraguayans into both Argentina and Brazil.

The birth rate. What happens to the traditionally very high birth
rates in most of the Latin American countries is, of course, the key
to what will happen to the increase of population in those countries
in the next few decades. Even with the very inadequate statistical
materials that are available, it is well established that the basic reason
for the present almost unprecedentedly high rates of population
growth is the persistence of extremely high birth rates, whereas since
about 1925 the also traditionally high death rates have plummeted
to relatively low levels.

In order to get before the reader such data pertaining to birth and
death rates in the various countries as are readily available, Table 3
has been prepared. It contains the best information that is to be had
for the various countries in the 1970s, and therefore, unfortunately,
the materials on the rates of reproduction of the peoples of Latin
America that usually are fed into the computers in demographic and
economic analyses of various kinds. However, if one merely compares the rates as published with the much more reliable information
on population trends and rates of growth as given in Table 1, materials derived largely from successive counts of the populations, it is
readily apparent that for most of the countries little or no credence
should be given to the reported birth rates. The alternative, however,
to using the data as published is the kind of detailed country-by-
country study such as formed the basis for the materials given in
Chapters 2 and 3 on Brazil and Colombia, respectively, and for most
of the countries in Latin America this kind of work is still to be done.

For present purposes, therefore, we can merely warn against placing any reliance on the rates that we, or anyone else for that matter,
may compute or estimate for many of the countries involved. In
Mexico and a few of the small countries such as the Dominican
Republic, El Salvador, Honduras, and Nicaragua, the reported rates

TABLE 3

Reported Birth Rates, Death Rates, and Rates of Natural Increase of
Population in the Latin American Countries

Country	Year	Birth Rate	Death Rate	Rate of Natural Increase
North America				
Costa Rica	1972	31.6	5.7	25.9
Cuba	1971	30.3	6.0	24.3
Dominican Republic	1970	40.1	6.0	36.1
El Salvador	1971	42.1	7.9	34.2
Guatemala	1972	42.5	9.4	33.1
Haiti	—	—	—	—
Honduras	1970	42.7	8.1	34.7
Mexico	1972	44.6	9.1	35.5
Nicaragua	1971	41.0	7.1	33.9
Panama	1972	34.5	5.7	28.8
South America				
Argentina	1968	22.6	9.5	13.1
Bolivia	1968	23.6	7.0	16.6
Brazil	—	—	—	—
Chile	1970	24.6	8.5	16.1
Colombia	1968	31.4	8.5	24.9
Ecuador	1971	38.7	10.1	38.6
Paraguay	1970	33.4	—	—
Peru	1967	32.0	7.6	24.4
Uruguay	1970	22.4	9.2	13.2
Venezuela	1972	38.6	6.6	30.2

SOURCE: Compiled and computed from data from the Inter-American Statistical Institute, "Situación Demográfica . . . ," *América en Cifras: 1974* (Washington, D.C.: Organization of American States, 1974), pp. 86–87, 105.

are less unrealistic than those for many of the others. But high as these are, they too probably are understatements. On the other hand, the comparatively low rates for Argentina and Uruguay may be fairly good reflections of the actuality. Except for these two countries, and to a lesser extent for Chile and Cuba, however, it is quite unlikely that the actual birth rates are less than 40; most of them, including those for the populous countries of Brazil, Colombia, Mexico, Peru, and Venezuela, are probably at least 45 births per year per 1,000 population. This means that the present extremely high rates of population growth in the Latin American countries are almost sure to continue for the next decade or so, and that substantial improvements will have to be made in their systems of agriculture (ways of farming, types of farming, and systems of distribution and marketing) if there is to be any rise in their standards and levels of living.

The death rate. Almost all of the death rates given in Table 3 probably are substantially too low. It is true that the coverage in the registration of deaths usually is somewhat more complete than that in the registration of births, but even so it is likely that large numbers of deaths also fail to figure in the national registers.

It should be stressed, however, that even though the reported death rates are in many cases highly questionable, the actual rates still are only fractions of what they were as late as 1940 or even 1950. It also is to be emphasized here, as in many other connections, that the recent precipitous reduction of the death rates, unaccompanied by any significant decrease in the birth rates, is what produced and continues the extremely high rates of increase of population in the Latin American countries. Even so, it appears almost certain that the rapid reduction of mortality that has taken place during the last quarter of a century has about exhausted the possibilities. Most of the results that can be achieved by fast, relatively inexpensive preventive measures (vaccinations, injections, the use of the "wonder drugs," programs to safeguard water and milk supplies, the installation of sanitary systems, etc.) already have been attained. Further reductions in the death rates will be neither easy nor inexpensive, and it will be extremely difficult to get any substantial results quickly. To reduce the death rates by another two points in the years immediately ahead may prove to be far less feasible than was the task of bringing them down by ten or fifteen points only twenty-five years ago. Moreover, if programs of family planning, rising standards and levels of living, the efforts of more and more couples to ascend in the socioeconomic scale, and so on, actually produce a fall in the birth rates, the decrease in the proportions of the population of less than fifteen years of age that this will effect itself will make for a substantial rise in the crude death rates.

The Immediate Outlook

Finally in this chapter an attempt is made to estimate or conjecture what the population of each country and that of Latin America as a whole will be in the immediate future, that is, in 1980. These definitely are not so-called projections, since no one standard formula has been applied, such as, for example, assuming that between 1970 and 1980 the population will grow at the same rate as that which took place between 1960 and 1970. Rather, a number of such projections have been made, and these have been checked against variations and trends in the birth and death rates in the countries for which the vital statistics are most reliable. Some allowances also have been made for some special events thought to influence the birth or death rates in some of the countries, so that the final figure in each case is our own best judgment or guess as to what the population will be in 1980. It should be stressed, however, that each nation has been studied as a unit, and that greater reliance was placed upon some of the factors in the process of arriving at a figure for a specific country than was true in the estimates given for some of the others. For example, in the case of Argentina, for which it is believed the statistics on the registration of births are fairly reliable, much more reliance was placed upon the reported trend in the birth rate than in the case of Colombia, for which the reported number of births are gross understatements.[2] The results of these estimates, along with the estimates of the rates of growth as they were in 1975, are given in Table 4.

In the interpretation of these materials at the present time, and also early in the 1980s after the results from the censuses taken about 1980 are known, it should be kept in mind that the completeness of the enumerations is an unknown that may seriously affect the calculations for past decades as well as estimates, projections, or forecasts of future populations. For example, prior to the 1960 census in Brazil, no one, in Brazil or out of it, was prepared to venture the proposition that Brazil's population in 1960 would be more than sixty-six million. Nevertheless, catching all of the experts by surprise, the enumeration of 1960 accounted for about seventy-one million people. To this day it is not known how much, if any, of the enormous increase was due to more complete census coverage in 1960 than in 1950, and how much of it represented an actual growth of population. Much the same can be said about the figures for some of the other countries. It also should be recalled that the problem of underenumeration also is a serious one in connection with the figures issued in the reports of the United States Bureau of the Census.

Only a few concluding observations are given relative to the data presented in Table 4. The first of these is that the rate of growth remains high, very high, during the 1970s, and that it is likely to continue that way on into the 1980s. For the area as a whole the figure of 2.8 percent per year, the estimated level in 1975, means that if continued the area will double its population again by 1990. Moreover, the rate remains very high in all of the more populous countries except Argentina. Second, the population of the twenty countries taken as a whole in 1975 amounts to about 10 percent of the estimated population of the entire world. In this connection it is well to keep in mind that at the opening of the twentieth century only about 2.7 percent of the world's population lived in Latin America.[3] Third, as the last quarter of the twentieth century opens there is at the close of each year about nine million more Latin Americans than there were at its beginning, a figure substantially higher than the combined populations of Panama, Costa Rica, Nicaragua, and Paraguay.

TABLE 4

Estimates of the Populations and Rates of Growth in 1975 and of the
Populations in 1980 of the Latin American Countries

| Country | Rate of Growth 1975 | Estimated Populations (000s) | | 1980 |
| | | 1975 | | |
		Number	Percent	Number
North America	3.0	94,200	30.7	107,600
Costa Rica	3.2	2,000	0.7	2,300
Cuba	1.8	9,200	3.0	10,100
Dominican Republic	3.0	4,600	1.5	5,200
El Salvador	3.0	4,000	1.3	4,600
Guatemala	3.0	5,500	1.8	6,300
Haiti	2.0	5,000	1.6	5,600
Honduras	3.1	2,900	1.0	3,300
Mexico	3.4	57,000	18.6	65,600
Nicaragua	3.0	2,300	0.7	2,600
Panama	3.2	1,700	0.5	2,000
South America	2.6	212,500	69.3	239,500
Argentina	1.5	25,000	8.1	26,700
Bolivia	2.7	5,000	1.6	5,600
Brazil	2.7	108,000	35.2	122,000
Chile	2.0	10,000	3.3	11,000
Colombia	3.2	24,200	7.9	28,000
Ecuador	3.3	7,000	2.3	8,100
Paraguay	3.0	2,700	0.9	3,100
Peru	3.1	15,000	4.9	17,200
Uruguay	1.2	3,100	1.0	3,300
Venezuela	3.3	12,500	4.1	14,500
Latin America	2.8	306,700	100.0	347,100

Fourth, and finally, it is unlikely that any dramatic drops in the rates of growth in any of the countries will take place in the immediate future, so that it probably is safe to "project" a rate of increase for the countries taken taken together of at least 2.7 percent well into the 1980s. This seems to be the reality facing all of those who attempt to help keep the increases in the production of food, feed, and fiber fast enough to at least prevent the level of living from being reduced and if possible to be substantially increased.

5

Current Population Trends of Special Importance for Planning in Latin America

The adequacy of present planning programs throughout Latin America will be determined to a considerable degree by the extent to which realistic appraisals of population trends figure as components in those programs. In this context, four specific demographic developments deserve special consideration. These are as follows: (1) the tremendous speed with which the population of the twenty Latin American countries is increasing; (2) the overwhelming extent to which the natural increase of the population in the various countries is being siphoned off from the rural districts and concentrated in and about the principal cities; (3) the strong tendency for the rural-urban migrants of lower-class status to aggregate in huge "bands of misery," or suburban slums, in the areas adjacent to cities, extensive areas occupied by squatters in which the work of "urbanization" has hardly begun; and (4) the failure of the numerous offsprings of the agricultural families to move into, conquer, and bring into production vast areas throughout Central and South America that still are lacking inhabitants.

Each of these will be discussed briefly in turn, but prior to that a few words of caution will be given pertaining to the uncritical adoption and use of expressions and ideas that, although they may from time to time gain widespread popularity in connection with demographic matters, are hardly entitled to pass as legal tender in any genuinely scientific discussion of population topics.

First published in *Demography India: Journal of the Indian Association for the Study of Population* 1, no. 1 (October 1972): 28–37, and republished here with the permission of the editors of that journal.

Demographic Sophisms Now Circulating Widely

Currently, the most startling example of the naïve acceptance and glib use of misleading demographic terms may be seen in the almost universal employment of the term population "explosion" as the designation for the present high rates of population increase. It hardly seems possible that this could have taken place were it not for the universal fears of mankind with respect to grave consequences that might accompany men's efforts to domesticate and control the atom. These facts apparently have enabled some of those who seek support for their proposed population policies to play upon the emotions of men and women rather than to appeal to their critical judgments, to produce an association in millions of minds between the fantastic destructiveness of unleashed atomic energy and the high rate of population increase. Actually, until the basic meanings of an entire family of words in all of the languages derived from Latin sources are altered radically, it would be difficult to discover a more inappropriate designation than that of "explosion" for the steady, prolonged, and rapid rate of population increase presently taking place in the world, and especially throughout Latin America. Were there actually to be a population explosion, the phenomenon would consist of one instantaneous, disruptive, and destructive release of pent-up energy, after which the pulverized remnants would all quickly return to their previous levels. Such a thought obviously is utterly ridiculous and inconceivable in anything having to do with population changes. Even a less radical figure of speech such as the eruption of a geyser hardly can appeal to critical minds as being appropriate in connection with the growth of human numbers. Rather, the population phenomenon resembles the rise of the water level in a tank in which two faucets (births within the area involved and migrations to it) add to the volume of the liquid and two outlets (deaths in the area involved and migrations from it) tend to decrease the amount of water in the tank. To continue this figure of speech, until recent decades throughout Latin America the faucet chiefly responsible for the addition of numbers (the birth rate) was wide open, resulting in a rate of inflow of from 45 to 50 per 1000 population per year; and the major outlet (the death rate) also was unobstructed so that from 35 to 40 persons per 1000 population were decimated annually. As a result, the population rose steadily but

with no great rapidity. Since 1925, however, the application of vaccinations, inoculations, the safeguarding of milk and water supplies,
and a host of other measures based upon the germ theory of disease
have greatly reduced the death rate, or, to follow our analogy, have
closed to a considerable extent the principal outlet of the tank. The
birth rate, though, has remained high, so that the inflow has continued unabated. As a result, the volume of liquid in the tank, or the
number of inhabitants, has continued to increase steadily and constantly, but now the rise is no longer slow. It is moving upward at
a very rapid rate. Let us stress, though, that there is nothing even
remotely resembling an explosion taking place, nor even an eruption
such as that of a geyser. Moreover, this is indeed fortunate for those
involved in planning programs, for if there were any basis for thinking of current population increase as an explosion, any attempts at
planning for or with the people of various cities, states, and nations
would be of the utmost futility. My point here is, of course, that all
of those involved in planning activities should use the same critical
faculties in connection with the concepts offered them by demographers that they employ in connection with the terms they must deal
with that come from geology, civil engineering, physics, chemistry,
and all the other sciences.

Another sophistic practice that is comparable to having counter-
feit coins pass as legal tender, particularly in planning circles, is the
tendency to think of population increase largely as an independent
variable instead of the dependent variable that it generally is. There
appear to be two principal reasons for this. First, there is the insatia-
ble appetite on the part of municipal, state, and national agencies for
speculations of any type with respect to what the population of the
administrative unit with which they are concerned will be ten,
twenty-five, or fifty years hence. Of course, were it possible to know,
or to estimate with any reasonable degree of accuracy, how many
people there would be in 1980, 2000, or 2025 in Buenos Aires or
Mexico City, the state of São Paulo or the provincia of Lima, in
Colombia, Venezuela, or any of the other countries, and so on, the
problems of planning would be reduced to a mere fraction of what
they actually are. Hence I fear there is a strong tendency for us to
substitute the wish for the reality, and to forget the fundamental fact
that the three factors (births, deaths, and migrations) whose combined effects produce observed population changes themselves are
the net products of hundreds of specific social, economic, and politi-

cal influences. We tend to think of the changes in the numbers of human beings principally as an antecedant and not as a consequent. Of course this is matched in other aspects of current social and economic theorizing such as that which seems almost to attribute volition of their own to such statistical indexes of the cumulative effects of hosts of influences as the "gross national product" or an indicator of price levels on the stock market.

As a result of this dubious way of thinking, of the failure in social and economic matters to distinguish between cause and effect, or at least to recognize that a given factor such as the changing number of inhabitants is fully as much, if not more, an independent as it is a dependent variable, the so-called population projections appear to be a *sine qua non* of planning projects. Thousands of people seem to be fascinated with the particular kind of "numbers game" this represents, and the variety of forms it takes is truly a thing of wonder. Actually, of course, the process calls for the minimum in the way of sophistication and the maximum in the way of repetitious, tedious arithmetical calculations. Always fundamental in the process is the *assumption* that *if* the rate of increase remains as it was during some period, or *if* the factors remain unchanged, or *if* the latter change in a certain way, *then* after the lapse of stated periods of time the population will be so and so.

For some curious reason, those who do, or who employ clerks to do, the thousands of simple arithmetical computations involved apparently feel no obligation to supply their clients with any indications of their best professional judgment, based on all of the knowledge that presumably they possess, as to what the population of a given center, state, or nation actually will be ten, twenty, or fifty years in the future. They merely present the results of the tedious computations as to what would be the case *if* their simple assumptions should prove to be correct. In reality this never, or almost never, proves to be the case. If anyone will take the trouble to compare the results of projections made ten, twenty, or thirty years in the past with the actual trends since those projections were published, the one thing that will prove crystal clear is that the projections never approximate the actual trends. Specifically, if the projection indicates that the population of a given territorial unit will be a given number in 1980, or 1990, or 2000, the one thing of which we may be sure is that such actually will not be the case. This is true even of the most elusive procedures of all, in which the "professional" passes on to the "layman" for the latter's own selection and use not just one but three or more "projections," dubbed variously as "high," "medium," "low," and so on. It is certain, though, that these dubious practices will continue until those in the planning profession develop a sophistication about population matters sufficient to cause them to refuse to accept such obvious counterfeits as "coin of the realm." As is probably apparent to those who read these words, I absolutely refuse to have any part in the making of population projections. I will, however, venture my best judgment, or estimate, of what the population of a given city, country, state, or nation will be at one or more dates in the immediate future, based upon my knowledge of the factors involved, the observed trends in each of them, and the changes in these factors that seem most likely to take place. Even so, since the fluctuations in the birth rate, which seem to be largely unpredictable, constitute the principal determinant in most of the equations for states and nations, I recognize that any such estimate is subject to a very large margin of error.

The Huge Upsurge in the Population

Nowadays, those writing about demographic subjects are employing a rich variety of superlatives to denote the rapidity with which the population is increasing in the world as a whole and its various subdivisions. Except for such spurious terms as "population explosion," these superlatives are more appropriately applied to what is taking place throughout Latin America than to the trends in any other large section of the earth's surface. All during the second quarter of the twentieth century, the growth of population in the twenty Latin American countries went on at a pace substantially greater than that for other great world regions, and considerably above the rates of increase in the Latin American nations themselves during the opening quarter of the century and those prevailing throughout the nineteenth and eighteenth centuries. Moreover, since 1950, the speed with which the population of Latin America has been growing itself has been on the increase, so that between 1950 and 1960 the coefficient of growth was higher than that for the period 1940 to 1950, and that for 1960 to 1975 promises to be even higher than the extremely high indexes previously attained.

Some statistical data properly used will help us to place the current rates of population growth in Latin America in their proper perspective. No attempt is made to go back farther than 1900, though, since prior to that date the lack of census data and the obvious inconsistencies in and unreliability of the various estimates blur the picture for the nineteenth and eighteenth centuries. When the twentieth century opened, however, it would seem that there were approximately 1,630 million persons on the earth, of whom about 43 million, or around 2.7 percent, were inhabitants of the twenty Latin American countries. Two decades later, or just after the close of the First World War, the world's total population had risen to some 1,811 million, while that of the Latin American nations had mounted even more rapidly to a total of about 89 million or fully 4.9 percent of all. After 1920 the health programs in the various parts of the world, aided immensely by the work of the Rockefeller Foundation, began to reduce the death rates substantially, and the pace at which the earth's inhabitants were increasing quickened considerably, so that by 1940 there probably were about 2,250 million living members of the human race. But again during this twenty-year period, the rate of population increase in Latin America greatly excelled that for the remainder of the world, so that by 1940 Latin Americans alone had come to number about 123 million, or 5.5 percent of the earth's inhabitants. The conflagration that afflicted the world between 1940 and 1950 slowed the rate of population increase to some extent but certainly did not halt it even in Europe and Asia, and probably did not affect it at all throughout Latin America. In any case, by 1950, when the total population of the world had grown to about 2,510 million, there were at least 154 million Latin Americans, or 6.0 percent of those alive at that date. Subsequently, during the decade ending in 1960, the number of people on the earth's surface shot upwards rapidly to a mark of 2,995 million, with the increase in Latin America still in the vanguard. Thus, in 1960 the combined population of the twenty countries involved was 202 million, and it accounted for 6.8 percent of all the people in the world. By 1970 the comparable figures were 276 million Latin Americans, constituting 7.7 percent of the world's population.

These materials may be summarized succinctly by indicating that in 1900 there was only one Latin American in every thirty-seven members of the human race, whereas by 1970 this ratio was one out of every ten. Thus a phenomenal change is under way, a change that constitutes a major challenge for all of us who have a responsibility in connection with the plans and policies for the future well-being of the people in the neighborhoods, communities, states, and nations in which we live. Moreover, this rapid increase of the population of the Latin American countries probably will continue until at least 1980, when a substantial decline in the birth rate may begin. In the near future, though, the proportion of Latin Americans in the world's population will continue to rise, probably to about one in every nine in 1980.

The rates of growth involved in the above discussion approximate, for Latin America as a whole, about 3 percent per year for the decade 1960 to 1970. This is my best judgment as to what the rate actually was, an index that has been by no means easy to establish. This in turn represents an upturn from one of about 2.5 for the decade ending in 1950. Moreover, one would be amiss were he to fail to mention that a rate of 3 percent per year is almost unprecedented for the population of any substantial portion of the globe on which we live. As far as can be ascertained, throughout the entire history of mankind no other extensive area on earth, with the single exception of the United States between 1790 and 1860, has previously experienced a rate of population growth equal to 3 percent per year. In terms of the numbers of additional human beings that must figure in the projects of those responsible for planning activities, this means that in the years that have just passed there have been more than eight million more Latin Americans alive at the end of a year than there were at its beginning.

Another feature of current population increases in Latin America is the extent to which the exceedingly high rates prevail throughout the many far-flung and widely divergent parts of Mexico and Central America, the three island republics, Brazil, and the Spanish-American parts of South America. Thus in Brazil, which alone contains more than one-third of the total population of the twenty countries and for which the reported increase as shown by the 1960 and 1970 censuses amounted to 30 percent, only six of the twenty-six states and other major civil divisions registered increases in population of less than 25 percent during the decade and eleven of them showed increases of over 35 percent. Mexico, the second most populous of the Latin American countries, experienced a 38.8 percent increase of population between 1960 and 1970. And current rates of growth are

above 3 percent per year in Costa Rica, the Dominican Republic, El
Salvador, Honduras, Nicaragua, Panama, Colombia, Ecuador, Peru,
and Venezuela. In the entire group comparatively slow growth of
population is exhibited only in Argentina and Uruguay, where the
present rates are about 1.5 and 1.2 percent per year, respectively.

The Dizzy Pace of Urban Growth

Despite the universality of high current rates of population increase in Latin America in terms of national and state units, a
startling redistribution of population is going on within each of the
countries and their principal subdivisions. In brief, the overwhelming part of the population increase is accounted for by the growth
of cities and towns. This is not because the rate of natural increase,
or the difference between births and deaths, in urban districts exceeds
that in the rural areas, for the opposite is the case; rather, it is chiefly
because a very large proportion of the children born and reared in
the rural districts are flocking into the state and national capitals,
and into other urban places, as soon as they reach the ages of early
adulthood. In this connection my studies in Brazil, Colombia, and
some of the other countries indicate that approximately two-thirds
of the increase of population in the urban districts is due to migration
from the rural areas.[1] But this rush to the cities is new. It would find
no place of importance in the projections of the populations of various cities made twenty-five years ago. Indeed, an interesting realm
for speculation and study is to be found precisely in the question as
to why, after centuries of existence as societies that were overwhelm-
ingly rural, agricultural, and pastoral in nature, the Latin American
countries suddenly were caught up in a mad rush to urbanize, indus-
trialize, and "modernize" almost literally overnight.

Rather than spending our limited space on speculations, though,
let us examine some of the most important data on the subject. At
mid century only about nineteen million, or 36.5 percent, of Brazil's
population were classified in the urban category. Nevertheless, between 1950 and 1970 her urban population increased by thirty-three
million, or by about 173 percent, whereas the rural population, in
this vast country where at least half of the national territory is
entirely or almost entirely devoid of inhabitants, increased by only
eight million, or 24 percent. Thus, during the latest two intercensal

periods, in the half continent called Brazil over 80 percent of the total increase of population took place in cities and towns, the most publicized feature of which, of course, was the phenomenal growth of the two great conurbations of Rio de Janeiro and São Paulo. Each of these presently contains at least seven million inhabitants, but the immense flow of people from the country to the city was by no means confined to these two gigantic centers.

Actually, on the relative basis, the burgeoning of such cities as Belo Horizonte, capital of Minas Gerais, with a population of 1,233,000 in 1970, and Fortaleza, capital of the great northeastern state of Ceará, with well over 840,000 inhabitants in 1960, was even more spectacular than the growth of Rio de Janeiro and São Paulo. Furthermore, both Recife and Salvador have grown so fast that each passed the one million mark prior to 1970, while the list of places having over half a million residents now includes not only Pôrto Alegre, with 886,000 inhabitants, but Belém, Curitiba, and Brasília as well. In addition, such places as Manaus, São Luís, Teresina, Natal, João Pessoa, Maceió, and Goiânia are meccas for so many of those who leave the rural districts that all of them have grown into cities having more than 200,000 residents. As a matter of fact, it must be stressed that in some areas, and especially in the much-publicized northeastern region of Brazil, that nation's problem area number one, the mushrooming of cities and towns was accompanied by almost no increase in the rural population. Between 1950 and 1960 percentage increases in the urban and rural populations, respectively, of most of the northeastern states and the major entities in the eastern region as well were as follows: Piauí, 75 and 10; Ceará, 66 and 10; Rio Grande do Norte, 71 and 1; Paraíba, 55 and 4; Pernambuco, 59 and 2; Alagoas, 50 and 4; Sergipe, 44 and 6; Bahia, 67 and 9; and Minas Gerais, 70 and 9. Nor was the situation much different in the other populous sections of the country. In the great southern state of Rio Grande do Sul an increase of 72 percent in the urban population was accompanied by one of only 9 percent in the rural population; in the state of Rio de Janeiro, the corresponding indexes were 90 percent and 10 percent, respectively; and in justly famed São Paulo, an increase of 3,346,000 (or 70 percent) in the urban population dwarfed in significance that of only 495,000 (or 12 percent) in the rural population. Moreover, when the details from the 1970 census become available they are almost certain to show even greater rural-urban differentials than these.

Such are a few of the most pertinent facts about the mushroom growth of cities in Brazil, the country for which the data are most satisfactory at the time these lines are written. Perhaps, though, one additional comment should be made. If Brazilian planners follow the pattern that is general throughout North and South America, that is to say if they concentrate their attention almost exclusively upon the problems of the urban centers to the neglect of the vast rural areas, they will still have many, many more towns and cities to take into account. In Brazil alone, places of 2,000 or more inhabitants increased from only 900 in 1940 to 1,174 in 1950 and to 1,799 in 1960, and it probably will not require another twenty years from the latter date for this number to double again.

Changes comparable to those in Brazil also took place in Mexico. As late as 1950, only 43 percent of her twenty-six million inhabitants fell in the urban category, but during the ensuing twenty years her urban population mounted by 140 percent whereas her rural population rose by a mere 35 percent. As a result, by 1960 Mexico had joined Argentina, Chile, and Venezuela in the small group of Latin American countries having predominantly urban populations. And by 1970 her urban population of 26,329,000 made up 56.8 percent of the total population. At the time of Mexico's 1970 census enumeration, the Federal District already was far too small to contain the huge built-up area of Mexico City, the capital. Nevertheless, it alone contained 6,874,000 inhabitants. Moreover, although between 1950 and 1970 the rate of growth in this immense city was 125 percent, it was less rapid than that for the nation's urban population as a whole, which indicates that the phenomenal increase in the number of residents of cities and towns was by no means limited to the capital. For example, between 1950 and 1970 the populations of three other major cities swelled as follows: Guadalajara, from 377,-016 to 1,195,000; Monterrey, from 333,422 to 858,000; and Puebla, from 211,331 to 402,000.

The data from Argentina's 1970 census are not yet available to me in the detail needed for the most meaningful analyses of current trends. By 1960, however, three-fourths of Argentina's population already fell in the urban category, and the entire urban population was highly concentrated in the immense city of Buenos Aires and the satellites just beyond its own limits. In fact, the data for the period 1947 to 1960 make it evident that the bulk of the growth of population took place in the huge crescent-shaped agglomeration of minor civil divisions (*partidos*) immediately adjacent to the capital city. During the intercensal period, the seventeen divisions in this area more than doubled in population, with the actual change being from a total of 1,741,000 in 1947 to 3,647,000 in 1960. Among the most spectacular increases were those in the following *partidos:* La Matanza, from 98,000 to 403,000 (309 percent); Merlo, from 20,000 to 135,000 (575 percent); Quilmes, from 123,000 to 318,000 (158 percent); and San Martin, from 270,000 to 541,000 (93 percent). It is almost certain that this great tendency of Argentina's people to concentrate in the urban areas within the perimeter to greater Buenos Aires was even more pronounced between 1960 and 1970 than it had been in the previous thirteen years.

During the 1970s Colombia is almost certain to replace Argentina as the third most populous of the Latin American countries, and in it, as in Brazil, Mexico, and Argentina, the redistribution of population now under way on a huge scale is concentrating the population in the major cities and the immense suburban bands of misery that surround them. Colombia's latest census was taken in 1964 and the latest intercensal period covers the years 1951 to 1964. During that time, the nation's population increased from 11,548,000 to 17,485, 000 (51 percent), with the growth in the head towns (*cabeceras*) of the countylike *municipios* being from 4,468,000 to 9,903,000 (105 percent) and that in the remainder, the strictly rural sections of the country, from 7,080,000 to 8,391,000 (19 percent). By 1964, 27.6 percent of the population resided in cities of 100,000 or more inhabitants. For the fifteen-year period, the annual rate of growth of population averaged 3.2 percent for the nation as a whole. During those years, the changes in the principal cities were as follows: Bogotá, from 715,000 to 1,697,000, 6.8 percent per year; Medellín, from 358,000 to 773,000, 6.0 percent per year; Cali, from 284,000 to 638,000, 6.3 percent per year; and Barranquilla, from 280,000 to 498,000, 4.5 percent per year. Since 1964, the growth of Colombia's major cities has been fully as spectacular as it was between 1951 and 1964.

Data for the other Latin American countries are not yet available to the degree to justify a continuation of this line of analysis. It is certain, though, that the tendency of the people to flock into cities of all sizes in the other countries has been fully as great as it has been in Brazil, Mexico, Argentina, and Colombia.

Suburban Slums That Spring Up Overnight

Although the statistical data needed for the most adequate type of demonstration are lacking and probably will never be gathered and collected in a thoroughly satisfactory manner, one may be fairly certain that the growth of population has been especially rapid on the outskirts of the cities. Indeed, the huge belts of misery and deprivation which surround all or almost all of the Latin American cities surely are growing far more rapidly than are the central cities themselves. As a matter of fact, the most appropriate figure of speech available for use in describing the rise of these *suburbios* is its likeness to the way in which toadstools spring up overnight. The lion's share of all these unwanted and unmanageable aggregations of population involve illegal squatting on public or private property. They feature the quick erection of huts and hovels that are entirely devoid of facilities for disposing of wastes from human bodies and with improvised kitchens. They are lacking all other services including light and water and are built according to no plan whatsoever; therefore, even on a very small scale they would constitute a challenge to planners of overwhelming dimensions. Given the magnitude with which these *barrios marginales* actually are springing up, the degree to which this aspect of urbanization (as the word is used in English, and particularly by sociologists and economists) is outrunning *urbanización* or *urbanização* (in the sense these words are used by architects, engineers, and those in charge of development projects throughout the Spanish-American countries and in Brazil) constitutes what now is probably the most important social or societal problem in Latin America.[2]

The Slow Pace of New Settlement

Here and there throughout Latin America an energetic thrust of new settlement is bringing an extensive area of virgin territory into cultivation and adding a broader base to the economies of some of the countries. In the 1970s, this is especially true in Brazil. But this is not general, and at the pace at which the occupation of the unsettled sections of South and Central America is going on, it will be centuries before large portions of Bolivia, Peru, Colombia, Venezuela, and some of the Central American countries will make any significant contribution to the welfare of mankind. Here again the lack of detailed information from two or more recent censuses limits greatly the scope of any studies that may be made of the phenomenon, but enough information is available to make crystal clear the lack of any comprehensive onslaught upon the uninhabited portions of Latin America. Fortunately, the information from the 1950 and 1960 censuses in Brazil has been tabulated with a promptness and attention to comparability of data for small territorial units that well might serve as a model for other countries to emulate. To benefit as much as possible by this information, the present writer has studied the redistribution of population in the rural sections of Brazil and on the basis of the tables and maps prepared, and a general knowledge of the distribution of population and population trends in Brazil, certain generalizations may be made. For the period 1950 to 1960, it is evident that the only portions of that great country in which there were any large and sustained efforts to bring new areas into production were the northern part of the state of Paraná; the north-central portion of Maranhão; the districts in Goiás that are fairly close to the new capital, Brasília; the Rio Doce Valley and the area just to the north of it in Minas Gerais; and the extreme northwestern section of São Paulo.

The changes in Brazil between 1960 and 1970 did not differ from those during the previous decade in any great respect except that the building of the road from Brasília, the new national capital, to Belém, great entrepôt of the immense Amazon Valley, attracted about two million people into the previously unoccupied zone adjacent to it. Perhaps this was the major stimulus that caused those who direct the fortunes of the huge half continent to launch the greatest road building and colonization efforts in the nation's history. In any case, in 1970 a gigantic undertaking to build a highway from the Atlantic Coast to the Peruvian border, an artery of transportation almost across the continent of South America at its widest part, was launched. This highway is designed to connect all of the heads of navigation on the southern tributaries of the Amazon River, and the zones on either side of it are to be settled with farmers on allotments of land of about 250 acres in size, all grouped about new villages, towns, and small cities. It is one of the most grandiose attempts to plan a redistribution of population that has ever come to my attention.

Elsewhere in Latin America there are thrusts of new settlement here and there into virgin territory, but extensive areas are still to be colonized. As in Brazil, the huge expanses of unsettled territory in the Spanish-American portions of the vast Amazon Basin offer tremendous opportunities for large numbers of well-prepared agricultural and nonagricultural people. The same is true of most of the territory drained by the Orinoco and the Paraguay rivers. It is my own considered opinion that within the next few decades huge populations will be attracted into these potentially fruitful regions. Therefore, as a conclusion to this chapter, I quote the judgment I expressed a few years ago about the development of the immense plains that lie to the east of the Andes and constitute very large portions of all the territory in Colombia and Venezuela: "I continue to believe that such projects as the construction of a modern highway built on almost a bee line from Caracas, Venezuela to Villavicencio, at the base of the Andes, a short distance to the east of Bogotá, Colombia, would be of as much consequence in the development of South America as the Aswan Dam will be in that of Africa."[3]

6

Some Emerging Issues in Population Policies in Latin America

Drastic changes presently are under way in the thinking about population matters on the part of those who occupy positions of authority and responsibility in the social, economic, political, and governmental realms throughout the various Latin American countries. The time has passed when mere growth of population, the more rapid the better, was accepted without challenge as an indication that all was well with affairs in any particular one of the twenty nations that make up the Latin American group. Nowadays demographic matters have become burning issues in many parts of the Western Hemisphere, as indeed they have in the world as a whole.

Logically the entire subject of population policy may be divided into two principal parts, that is, that of a quantitative nature and that of a qualitative type. The first of these pertains to all measures that affect numbers of inhabitants, their distribution and redistribution, and their rates of increase or decrease; the second deals with ways and means of affecting the characteristics of the people involved such as marital condition, educational accomplishments and technical skills, health and physical stamina, and so forth. Obviously, however, for present purposes only a few aspects of either of these can be considered, and I have chosen to restrict my comments to those relating to the numbers, distribution, and growth of population.[1] This restriction means that we limit our consideration of population policy in Latin America to the ways and means of affecting or controlling the three factors that alone can have any direct bearing upon the number of people in any country, their distribution, and

First published in the *International Review of Modern Sociology* 3, no. 1 (March 1973): 25–30, and republished with the permission of Dr. Man Singh Das, editor of the *Review.*

changes in the same. As previously noted, these are, in order of their importance, births, deaths, and migrations. In considering them, however, we deal first with deaths, largely because that subject can be dismissed with a word; then we comment briefly upon policies respecting immigration, emigration, and internal migration; and we conclude with an examination of policies relating to the birth rate.

Mortality

The tremendous reduction in the death rates that has been accomplished throughout Latin America during the last twenty-five or thirty years is of course the factor directly responsible for the present burgeoning of population throughout the immense area extending from Mexico to Chile and Argentina. Furthermore, additional control over mortality in extensive sections of Latin America, such as the Brazilian Northeast where infant and other death rates still are high, may be expected to make further substantial contributions to the growth of population throughout the area. The value systems that the various Latin American societies share with most other parts of the world being as they are, however, it is unlikely that in my time or yours any proposed policies intended to produce an increase in the death rate or even those designed to restrict endeavors to reduce it still further will receive the slightest consideration. Life is considered to be better than death, and that is that! This dictum prevails now and almost certainly will continue to be the rule in the years to come. Even "mercy killings" of hopeless incurables and the failure to make every effort to extend the lives of those on the verge of death are condemned by the values of all the societies we are considering. Unlike the situation that has prevailed in some parts of the world, even infanticide is not an acceptable technique of population control in Latin America, and it is not likely to become one any time in the immediate future. Further reductions in the death rates of all the Latin American countries may be anticipated.

Migrations, International and Internal

Present and potential population policies involving measures for stimulating, prohibiting, controlling, or directing the movement of people from one place to another are much more complicated than those pertaining to mortality. All of the countries have in effect policies designed to control immigration from other parts of the world, and even the traditional practice of allowing almost complete freedom of movement of people between neighboring Latin American countries is giving rise to serious repercussions. Indeed, one Latin American nation (Cuba) has even placed stringent restrictions upon the freedom of egress. Moreover, within the various countries the solution of the problem of the rural "exodus," or the mass movement of people from the farms to the cities, is a matter of primary concern. We consider briefly policy matters related to four aspects of this general subject, namely, immigration from overseas, the exchange of population between the Latin American countries themselves, freedom of egress, and internal migrations.

Immigration from Other Parts of the World

With few exceptions at the present time severe restrictions upon immigration from Europe, Asia, and Africa are the order of the day in each of the Latin American countries. Even Argentina and Brazil, which long were the recipients of huge numbers of immigrants from Europe and, in the case of Brazil, from Japan, no longer permit the freedom of ingress which once was the rule. In the case of Brazil, however, the restrictions do not apply to immigrants from Portugal. In addition, other countries such as Venezuela, which accepted large numbers of European immigrants during the years immediately after the close of the Second World War, have reimposed severe limitations upon immigration. From the standpoint of the number of people and the growth of population, however, it makes comparatively little difference whether immigration policy is liberal or restrictive. With a very few exceptions, such as the recent case of Israel, immigration has never been a major factor in the growth of a nation's population. Even in the United States, Brazil, Canada, Australia, and New Zealand, the countries that have been on the receiving end of the bulk of the international movements of the world's people, it is doubtful that immigration ever accounted for more than about 10 percent of the increase of population during any twenty-five-year period of time. Therefore, it is highly unlikely that any changes in general immigration policies that may be forthcoming in the near future in any Latin American country will have much effect upon the growth of its population. It should not be overlooked, however, that even a few thousand immigrants may be the means of implanting in a given country agricultural and industrial skills and systems that are of utmost importance in increasing the production of goods, fiber, and manufactured products, thus helping the means of subsistence to keep pace with the growth of population. This is to say that certain immigration policies may do much to enhance the well-being of people in a given society even though they have relatively little effect upon the growth of population in the same. Indeed, to the extent that a rather magical reliance upon *diffusion* as the means whereby socio-cultural traits, complexes, and systems get from one country to another is replaced by a knowledge that such inanimate things do not move under their own volition but must be carried and transplanted by human beings, well-planned immigration policies may contribute greatly to the process of development throughout Latin America.

Emigration and Immigration between Latin American Countries

Throughout most of Latin America there is at least tacit agreement that almost unrestricted flow of the nationals of one country across its boundaries with others will be permitted, and this type of international exchange of population goes on in considerable volume. Unfortunately, however, this important demographic process has received very little attention by those who study and write about social, economic, and demographic matters in the Americas, and there are no comprehensive statistics on the subject. Indeed, a few years ago when I presented a brief paper on the subject to the General Assembly of the International Population Union, I was unable to discover even one general treatment of this variety of immigration and emigration, although I did discover a few titles having to do with the movement of people from one Latin American nation to another.[2]

Among the things I called attention to in that paper were the immigration of Haitians to Cuba and the movement of people from El Salvador to Honduras. More recently the second of these has produced a brief but bloody conflict between two neighboring countries and has been the cause of grave concern to statesmen throughout the Western Hemisphere. Probably we need not say more in order to indicate that the time is coming when the various Latin American countries must attend explicitly to policies governing the movement of their nationals from one country to another.

Policies with respect to the importation of laborers for seasonal work in agriculture also constitute an important portion of the general problem of migrations between the various Latin American countries and of the relations of some of those countries, especially Mexico, with the United States. In no small numbers, workers from Chile go each year to participate in the picking of fruit crops in the Río Negro section in Argentina, and those from Bolivia find seasonal employment in the harvesting of sugar cane in northern Argentina. Thousands of laborers from Paraguay annually spend about half of the year in collecting and processing the maté twigs and leaves in southern Brazil. No doubt dozens of other examples of the ebb and flow of seasonal workers across the boundaries between the several Latin American countries could be added by those most familiar with life and labor throughout the hemisphere. Regulations governing such migrations and the ways in which they are enforced are likely to become increasingly important as matters of population policy in the decades immediately ahead.

Freedom of Egress

Whether or not the citizens of Latin America shall have the right to leave their homelands is an item of population policy that also seems to be calling for more attention than it has received in the past. Undoubtedly, for a long while many of those who have seized control of the governments in one way or another have sought to prevent their enemies, who often had been their oppressors, from fleeing to other parts of the world. More recently, however, the case of Cuba, where hundreds of thousands already have fled their native land, considerable numbers of others have perished in the attempt to do so, and other hundreds of thousands are searching for ways and means to flee, brings this matter into focus as never before has been the case in the Americas. Indeed, it seems to be a problem calling not only for national attention but for hemispheric and even general international consideration as well.[3] Perhaps even the Organization of American States (OAS) should develop explicit statements of principles involved, and the same would be true of the United Nations were such guidelines to have the slightest chance of avoiding the veto in the attempted actions of that body.

Internal Migrations

As one discusses national problems with leaders of government, education, commerce, industry, and agriculture in various parts of Latin America, certain aspects of internal migration are almost sure to figure prominently in the conversations. This is because the effects of rural-urban migration (both in the flight of agricultural laborers from the fields and ranches and the congregation of the migrant families in great urban and suburban slums), the problems connected with the colonization and settlement of frontier areas, the movement of families from farm to farm and from one region to another, and various other aspects of internal migration are almost constantly in the thoughts of those responsible for the social, economic, educational, and political affairs of the nations. Frequently, very frequently indeed, one hears the opinion that the movement from rural to urban areas ought to be prohibited, that many of the migrants should be returned to the rural districts from whence they came, and so on. As yet, however, with the exception of Cuba, no American government has sought to regiment workers and dispatch them to the parts of the country in which the planners decide their efforts are needed; hopefully such a state of affairs will be avoided in the years to come. Nevertheless, the formulation and establishment of more adequate policies with respect to internal migrations is of considerable importance in all of the countries we are considering.

From the little I personally have been able to learn about this subject, however, the greatest needs are for actions that will influence the voluntary movements of the people rather than direct actions to regulate internal migratory movements as such. By this I mean that the best ways to influence rural-urban migrations, the efforts to push forward the frontier, the often aimless shifting of farm laborers from one farm to another, and so on, are indirect. They necessitate much greater and better-directed efforts in the educational field, in connection with the land system (the nature of surveys and titles, the control of speculation in undeveloped lands, land tenure, systems of taxation, etc.), and in the development of an adequate system of agricultural credit, the improvement of the marketing system, and a vast extension of industrial plants. In other words, the way to control and direct internal migration is neither through policies designed to restrict the freedom of people to move from one place to another nor those that would force workers to go where the planners think they are needed. Rather, it is through policies that would increase the opportunities of those in the labor force and enhance the standards and levels of living of the workers and the members of their families. This calls for much greater efforts to bring about a balanced development of agriculture and industry, to promote trade and commerce, to develop more adequate educational and administrative systems, and to promote community development.

Family Planning and Birth Control

Of all the great changes during the last couple of decades in the matters with which leading Latin Americans have been preoccupied, none has been more dramatic than that with respect to the birth rate and what should be done about it. In 1951, aided financially by a fellowship from the John Simon Guggenheim Memorial Foundation, I spent four months visiting census and other statistical offices in every one of the twenty countries. This was for a small monograph that I hoped to do on the population of Latin America. At that time I took care to raise with the officials with whom I dealt, and also with the leading social scientists and other intellectuals with whom I conversed, the subject of the birth rate and what measures, if any, were being taken to promote family planning or birth control of any type. I want to stress, however, that only in Mexico and on the part of my long-time friend Manuel Gamio did I encounter anyone among the hundreds with whom I talked who exhibited the slightest interest in the topic or considered it to be of any particular significance in the society of which he formed a part. Dr. Gamio, though, indicated that from his own married daughters and their friends he knew the economic problems with which Mexican couples of the upper middle class were faced, and he also was aware of the head-on clash with deeply imbedded religious values that was produced by most ways and means of limiting the number of children. Moreover, he attributed much of the weakening influence of the church upon the women to this factor. But he alone among those I interviewed sensed the importance of the topic. Elsewhere the attitude generally was the same as that I long had encountered in Brazil, which as early as 1946 had caused me to specify that the refrain of Brazil's "theme song" was *falta de braços* or "lack of arms (hands)."[4] In brief, less than twenty-five years ago almost no one in the Latin American countries was concerned with national policies, or the lack of them, on anything related to family planning or the control of fertility.

How drastically all of this has changed since 1951! Almost all well-educated people in Latin America have at least heard the grossly inappropriate expression "population explosion," and not a few of them have come to think of rapid population increase as a national ill rather than a national asset. By the thousands Latin Americans in positions of authority and responsibility also recognize that the recent huge upsurge in population is due to a drastic reduction in mortality without any corresponding decrease in the rate of reproduction, and a large proportion of these leaders have become convinced that national population policies that will greatly reduce the annual number of births are the order of the day. To a major extent, of course, the issue arises in a realm that only a short time ago was generally governed by the religious and moral values emanating from the church, an area that rather suddenly has been transformed into one in which the state perforce must play a major role. This, in turn, has been facilitated, and possibly in some cases even precipitated, by the crisis with respect to authority within the church itself, but it also has waxed as endeavors to plan and promote development plans of one kind or another in various parts of Latin America have increased. Indeed, questions related to national policies with respect to family planning and birth control are now by far the most important demographic issues with which the governments of the twenty Latin American countries are confronted.

PART IV

Obstacles to Increased Production of Food

It is well established that most of the Latin American countries contain vast unused or slightly used resources of land, water, and other natural features needed in the production of food, feed, and fiber. Hence, the fact that such production has lagged sadly in many of the countries indicates rather clearly that various institutional or sociocultural factors must be responsible for the relatively poor showing. Three studies of these aspects of the race between population and the food supply are presented in this part. The first is a statement prepared at the request of the chairman of the Committee on Foreign Relations, the U.S. Senate, on the problems of agriculture in Latin America; the second is an analysis of the dead weight of the large latifundia in Brazil, first published in *Ceres,* an organ of the Food and Agriculture Organization of the United Nations; and the third is a lengthy treatment of the almost eternal conflict between the agricultural and the pastoral ways of life, a conflict that is a factor of tremendous importance in the development, or lack of it, in enormous portions of Latin America.

7

Problems of Agriculture in Latin America

Senator Morse and members of the subcommittee, it is a pleasure to participate to some extent in your "Survey of the Alliance for Progress" by appearing here this morning to comment briefly upon the study by Professors Thiesenhusen and Brown and to give a few of my own ideas about the more important current agricultural problems of the twenty Latin American nations, and I should stress that I have considered problems more than solutions.

Permit me to begin by indicating that I find very little in the report of my colleagues from the University of Wisconsin with which I am not in full agreement. The frame of reference they use is, of course, that of the agricultural economist, whereas I myself am a sociologist by profession. However, they themselves emphasize that "the tools of economics are insufficient to explain the complex process of development," and they devote one section of their brochure to "The Need for Institutional Change."

Inasmuch as I refer in my remarks to the results of some of my own studies, I am appending in a note, as a supplement to the bibliography prepared by Drs. Thiesenhusen and Brown, the titles of some of my own publications which bear directly upon the matter before the subcommittee.[1]

This statement was prepared at the request of Senator J. W. Fulbright, chairman, Committee on Foreign Relations, U.S. Senate, and was presented at a meeting of the Subcommittee on American Republics Affairs on Tuesday, February 27, 1968. Along with the questions and answers at this meeting of the subcommittee, its full text is published in the *Survey of the Alliance for Progress*, Senate Document No. 91–17, 91st Cong., 1st sess. (Washington, D.C.: U.S. Government Printing Office, 1969), pp. 250–97.

Population Problems

The first of the subjects which I discuss is population problems. I fully support the highly significant statements by Professors Thiesenhusen and Brown relative to population trends and problems in Latin America. Indeed it is with difficulty that I restrain myself from entering into a lengthy exposition of this subject, since, among other things, recently at the request of the Select Committee on Western Hemisphere Immigration I completed a study of "The Growth of Population in Central and South America, 1940 to 1970." I want to stress, though, that my conclusions, practically all of them, are fully in accord with the materials prepared for this subcommittee, except that the latter indicate that the lowest annual rate of increase is 1.3 percent for Uruguay, whereas my own figure for that country is substantially higher, or 1.8 percent.

The senators also may be interested in a couple of additional points. First, my own studies show that of approximately 71,000,000 people enumerated in Brazil's census of 1960, more than 7,000,000, or about one person out of ten, personally had moved from the rural districts to urban places during the decade ending in 1960. Moreover, there is nothing to indicate that this exodus has slowed appreciably since 1960. Second, I wish to present a few of the results of a study of depopulation in Colombia recently completed and submitted as a master's thesis at the University of Florida. This was done by Professor Carlos Escalante of Colombia's National University. This careful analysis of changes during the intercensal period 1951 to 1964 showed that almost 20 percent of all the countylike political subdivisions called *municipios* had fewer inhabitants in 1964 than they had thirteen years earlier.

Professor Escalante also sought to bring his data to bear upon another significant topic, the effect of mechanization (or motorization) of agriculture upon the need for workers in the agricultural districts. Admittedly, the procedures he had to use were rather crude and inadequate, but he was able to demonstrate that there was no correlation between the introduction of tractors for use on the farms and the increase or decrease of the rural population. In some areas the adoption of this source of power was accompanied by a falling off in the numbers of people in the rural districts, but in others exactly the opposite was true. This he explained as follows: In those sections in which the land was actually being used for the production of crops, the substitution of the tractor and attached implements for the traditional hand tools and hoe culture resulted in substantial displacement of workers. But, on the other hand, in extensive areas including large segments of the most fertile and most favorably located lands, the introduction of the tractor actually meant the substitution of tillage and the growing of crops for the traditional rudimentary pastoral economy of the nation. The result was a substantial increase in the need for workers, and hence a significant increase in the population.

"Inversion" of Land Use

Now, with that said, I will turn to point two in my own presentation, which is the curious "inversion" of land use with the pastures in the valleys and cultivated farms on the hillside.

At the time of the conquest of America, Spain was not an agricultural country, but one in which the livestock interests ruled supreme. The conquistadores quickly seized the best lands, the fertile plains which the native Indians were cultivating foot by foot in order to grow the crops of corn, potatoes, beans, and other crops on which their livelihood depended, and transformed these into pastures for their horses and cattle. The pigs which functioned as the commissaries for the bands of explorers and conquerors also served as the spear points of the attacks upon the Indians' cornfields and potato patches. This forced the natives to "abandon" their traditional fields, which in keeping with the king's orders made them legally eligible for assignment to members of the expeditions.

In this manner in many densely populated areas the Spaniards quickly took over for their own pastoral activities the larger portions of what had been the cultivated lands of the Indians, and the subjected natives were forced to make their plantings on the steep slopes —which never should have been cultivated—in the coves and other out-of-the-way places not wanted by the overlords. In many places such as the great savanna of Bogotá, the extensive coastal plains along the Caribbean, and the fabulously fertile Cauca Valley in Colombia, this merely meant putting into "cold storage" the best lands in the country; and since the close of the Second World War some of them again are being used to grow crops. However, in Peru, where the Incas had spent thousands of years applying advanced engineering skills and enormous amounts of labor in terracing the precipitous mountainside and perfecting an irrigation system to water their almost vertically superimposed fields, the results were tragic to the extreme. There European masters made no attempt to expand the agricultural base of the civilization; but their herds quickly destroyed large parts of it. Almost from the moment when their livestock were allowed to range about at will, here and there a few stones were loosened from one of the retaining walls of the restraining terraces, some of the canals became blocked at various places, and the waters began spilling out of their prepared channels and down the mountainside. Today we see the results—a major part of the great engineering achievements of the Incas have been irredeemably destroyed by the gulley erosion on a horrendous scale.

Concentration of Land Ownership

The third is the concentration in the ownership and control of the land and the problem of large, poorly managed farms, plantations, and ranches. The process just described whereby in many of the most densely populated parts of the New World the Spaniards seized the cultivated lands of the Indians and converted them into pastures for livestock was largely responsible for another of the great agricultural problems of the Latin American countries. This is the high degree to which the ownership and control of the land is concentrated in the hands of the members of a few affluent families. Indeed, this maldistribution of the property rights to the land, which existed almost unchallenged for over four hundred years, has been since 1950 the most burning issue in Latin America. In Mexico the upheaval began about 1917. It is the central feature of the agitation, proposals, plans, and programs for what most Latin Americans persistently designate as "agrarian reform." (For a list of the principal features of the hacienda system, see Chapter 3, pages 38–41.)

Defective Land Surveys and Titles

Most Latin American countries are severely handicapped in their efforts to solve their agricultural problems by the defective systems

used in surveying the boundaries of farms and ranches and recording
the titles to the same. Briefly stated, the surveys are both indefinite
and indeterminate, and most of the markers used are impermanent.
The result in many of the countries—such as Brazil and Colombia
—is quarrels, conflicts, and protracted lawsuits on a scale comparable to those which eventually forced Daniel Boone and many of his
contemporaries to move on west to Missouri. The property lines run
from stone to stone. They follow this or that watercourse or drywash.
Frequently, they are described as following the divide between two
streams. And often the land of Mr. A is described as bounded on one
side by the property of Mr. B, while conversely B's land is described
as being bounded in part by Mr. A's land. In the deeds it is almost
universal practice to state the area and then to qualify it by adding
the words *más o menos,* or more or less. All of this is complicated
to the extreme by plagues of squatters—simple country folk who seek
some place in which they can make small crops of corn, beans,
manioc, potatoes, yams, and so on, with which to feed their families
—who infest extensive areas in Central America, Colombia, Venezuela, Ecuador, Brazil, Peru, and some of the other countries.

In order to illustrate the seriousness of this problem, let me mention a few specific facts. First, the seriousness of this problem was the
reason I was sent to Colombia in 1943 by the U.S. Department of
State at the request of Dr. Miguel López Pumarejo, the director of
Colombia's National Credit Agency (the Caja de Crédito Agrario)
and brother of Alfonso López, then serving his second term as president of Colombia. Second, during the first three years of its existence,
a period ending in June 1965, Colombia's new Agrarian Reform
Institute retrieved for the public domain, through exercising the
right of eminent domain to lands illegally being held in estates of
2,000 hectares or more in size or merely by the "owners" surrender-
ing lands without the institution of lawsuits, a total of 1,327,225
hectares.[2] Multiply by about two and one-half in order to get acres.
Third, I wish to refer to a case in which the problem of clouded land
titles was solved, as given in the words of Dr. Hilgard O'Reilly
Sternberg, Brazil's most accomplished geographer, now a professor
at the University of California, Berkeley:

Take, for instance, the matter of clear-cut titles of ownership.
A profitable lesson can be learned from what is perhaps the

most successful of all large-scale pioneering settlement ventures
in Brazil—that carried out by a railroad and colonization company in northwestern Paraná state. In order to guarantee future
purchasers clear title to the land, the enterprise bought up all
titles presented—even if it meant—as it did—acquiring the
same tract five to six times.[3]

Fourth, and finally, let me mention the case of Brasília. Today
there is in the courts of Brazil the largest case in that nation's history.
According to the *Correio da Manha,* one of Brazil's leading daily
newspapers, of April 23, 1961, there were scattered throughout Brazil some forty thousand plaintiffs all claiming to be owners of parts
of the land on which the new capital city had been built. Together
they were demanding an indemnity of 120 billion *cruzeiros*—about
$425 million.

Wasteful, Inefficient Ways of Farming

The continued reliance upon antiquated ways or techniques of
farming certainly deserves mention in any list, however brief, of the
current problems of agriculture in Latin America. Drs. Thiesenhusen and Brown have pointed to some of these, and I desire to
supplement what they have said. Let me begin by indicating that as
we meet here this morning, when mankind is well within the portentous portals of the nuclear age, tens of millions of Latin America's
farmers still are relying upon ways of preparing seedbeds, caring for
the crops, taking the harvest, and transporting things on the farm
and from farm to market that are in no way more advanced than
those used in Babylonia during the days of Hammurabi. At that time,
those using the fertile flood plains of the Tigris and Euphrates, and
also the agriculturists in the valley of the Nile, were already at the
stage in which they were adding to the strength of their arms by the
use of a crude wooden plow, the lumbering ox, and practical applications of the principle of the wheel. A comparable degree of modernization of agricultural procedures has not yet been attained by
perhaps as many as one-half of all the Latin Americans who depend
upon agricultural activities for a livelihood. (For a classification and
discussion of ways of farming, see Chapter 12, pages 159–76.)

Defective Types of Farming

To the members of a subcommittee whose distinguished membership includes three senators from states that are entirely or partially within our fabulously productive corn belt I take especial pleasure in presenting my next point. Let me start by saying that I have observed carefully during a period of more than twenty-five years in areas extending from the Rio Grande to Patagonia and I have searched diligently through thousands of books, monographs, articles, et cetera, dealing with agriculture and animal husbandry and other aspects of life and labor in Latin America, but I have been unable to find a single case in which corn has been used for the purpose of fattening beef cattle. Almost the same can be said about the failure to use this economically golden grain for fattening hogs, although in some of the German settlements in southern Brazil the growth and feeding of corn is the basis for an important production of pork and pork products. I also know a few areas in Central America in which swine are allowed to "hog down" the corn as well as the plantains that are grown for that specific purpose. I consider this, which in effect means the lack of the demonstrably most effective combination of Latin America's three traditional farm enterprises—the growing of corn, the farrowing and fattening of swine, and the production of beef cattle—to be an outstanding example of agricultural underdevelopment in the twenty countries we are considering. It is my considered opinion that Argentina's marvelous pampas are fully as capable of supporting a prosperous corn–hog–beef-cattle type of farming as is Illinois, Iowa, Kansas, or Nebraska. There are numerous other extensive areas throughout South America, Central America, and Mexico which, although not as richly endowed with fertile soils and favorable climate as Argentina, likewise would benefit tremendously by a proper combination of the three farm enterprises which comprise the hard core of this type of farming.

It will be a happy day for many of the countries we are considering when, in the words of Thomas Nixon Carver, one of the most distinguished economists ever to fill a chair at Harvard University, "owing to the practice of allowing hogs to fatten on the droppings of the corn-fed cattle pork came [comes] to be, in a measure, a by-product of the beef-producing industry."[4] Or when (in the words of the man

of letters and the authority on animal husbandry who recently attempted a definitive study of pigs and history) the caption of a
photograph showing beef cattle and hogs together in a pasture in
Argentina, or Brazil, or Colombia, or one of the other countries can
truthfully read: "The base of corn-belt feed lot profits—hogs following steers"[5] and especially when one or more agricultural experiment
stations in Latin America will have data, similar to those painstak-
ingly assembled at the Iowa State Agricultural Experiment Station,
which show that "in 120 days of feeding, an average pig, following
two steers, picked up the equivalent of 312 pounds of corn."[6] I make
these statements even though I am fully aware that the feeding of
livestock in the United States is moving into a stage in which it no
longer is advisable, in many cases, to feed corn in the kernel or on
the cob directly to beef cattle, or to depend solely upon the gastric
processes of the steer to prepare corn for consumption by pigs. At
a few favored locations in Latin America undoubtedly it would be
advisable to attempt these most advanced features of animal husbandry. In extensive areas, however, and especially those removed
from markets, lacking adequate transportation facilities, and where
the farmers do not possess sufficient capital, the transplantation of
the system which prevailed in our great corn belt from about 1820
to 1960 is greatly to be desired.

Finally, I have been unable to discover anywhere in Latin America
a highly symbiotic relationship between the growing of rice of the
"paddy" or irrigated type and the production of beef cattle. I mention this because, as far as I have been able to determine, in Louisiana
the only effective way so far found to control the problem of red rice
is to plant that grain only in alternate years and to have beef cattle
graze the fields heavily in the "off years." Much to my dismay,
however, on a recent visit (for an entirely different purpose) to Cali,
Colombia, I was informed by my friend Dr. Victor Patiño, who
probably is Colombia's most accomplished agriculture scientist, that
the production of rice in the fabulously fertile Cauca Valley is on the
verge of extinction. The reason? The problem of red rice. Senator
Morse, in view of what I have said about the absence of these two
examples (the corn–hog–beef-cattle and the rice–beef-cattle combinations of enterprises), I hope you and the other members of the
subcommittee will think that I have some reason for mentioning
defective types of farming as one of Latin America's serious agricultural problems.

8

The Dead Weight of Latifundia

In the 1970s Brazil is taking enormous and unprecedented strides in the production of food, feed, and fiber. Despite the fact that her population is burgeoning (probably at a rate of about 3 percent yearly), the increase in the means of subsistence is moving even more rapidly, so that per capita consumption gradually is moving upward. Nevertheless, the increases are reflected on a very low base, so that the bulk of her huge rural population is still very poorly paid, fed, clothed, and housed. (Or to put it in more common terms, hired farm labor is abundant, cheap, and widely used, even though many millions of humble country people recently have flocked into Brazilian cities and towns.) For an enormous number of rural Brazilians, whose aspirations (or standards of living) have risen tremendously since 1950, the improvements being accomplished are agonizingly small and slow, or, in brief, the difference or gap between their standard of living and their level of living—the zone of exasperation —is expanding greatly.

Attention is directed in this article to the institution that has been largely responsible for the unenviable condition of Brazil's rural masses in the past. I also contend that it continues to obstruct substantially the development of the nation's agriculture. Furthermore, it also continues to prevent an equitable distribution of the product that is obtained from the soil among all those who have a part in agricultural and pastoral activities, and, in the last analysis, it precludes a substantial rise in the level of living, or improvement

First published in *Ceres* (FAO Review) 4, no. 5 (Sept.–Oct. 1971): 59–65, and reproduced with the permission of A. Biro, editor-in-chief.

in the way of life, of a very large segment of the Brazilian population. This is the system of large landed estates, which in Brazil is the equivalent of a system of very large farms, plantations, ranches, and largely unused private holdings that the Brazilians call latifundia. Any system of large landed estates means, of course, that there is a very high degree of concentration in the ownership and control of the land. It constitutes a genuine sociocultural system, that is, a functional set of various human, social, and cultural components, and in this case, it influences drastically the life and labor of the men, women, and children who are involved in this large, extremely symbiotic, and highly integrated arrangement.

With some notable exceptions, principally the areas in the three southern states (Paraná, Santa Catarina, and Rio Grande do Sul) inhabited by descendants of small farmers from Europe who were settled there in the latter part of the nineteenth century, Brazil's immense rural territory is dominated by the large landed estate. In some sections these huge properties are devoted to large-scale monoculture featuring the production of either coffee, sugar cane, or cacao, but for the most part the land is held in huge, very extensively used tracts on which an extremely rudimentary pastoral economy is the rule, so that the holdings qualify fully for the designation of latifundia, or great unused or poorly used properties, in the true Brazilian sense of the term. Such a society offers a rewarding specimen for study by a social scientist such as myself who seeks to determine what is actually responsible for the almost creature level of existence that has been the lot of the bulk of mankind from ancient times to the recent past and that remains the condition of a billion or so human beings in the 1970s.

Before proceeding with the analysis of the effects of the very high degree to which the ownership and control of farm and ranch land in Brazil is concentrated in a few hands, it seems advisable to present a few basic statistics that demonstrate conclusively the fact that the concentration still exists. One of the requirements of Brazil's new "Estatuto da Terra," put into effect in 1964, was that each proprietor supply the Instituto Brasileiro de Reforma Agrária with specific data about his holding or holdings. These data have been summarized and are available to the public in recent issues of the *Anuário Estatístico do Brasil.* They are far more satisfactory than earlier materials collected in the various censuses of agriculture, although few if any of the conclusions reached on the basis of the earlier materials have to be changed to be in accord with the data gathered in the recent nationwide inventory. The information is for the year 1967 and it shows the following: 36.4 percent of the proprietors have holdings of less than 10 hectares and these contain only 1.7 percent of the privately owned land; 41.6 percent of the proprietors, with holdings of from 10 to 49 hectares, have 10.1 percent of the land; 9.4 percent of the proprietors, with holdings of from 50 to 99 hectares, own 6.9 percent of the land; 11.2 percent of the owners, with holdings between 100 and 999 hectares, hold 32.4 percent of the land; 1.3 percent of the owners, with estates of from 1,000 to 9,999 hectares, possess 33.1 percent of the land; and 0.1 percent of the proprietors, whose holdings range upwards from 10,000 hectares, own 15.8 percent of the land. Few comments about these facts are needed, but it may be germane to state that in 1967 a mere 1.4 percent of those who by law were required to supply information on their landholdings possessed almost half (48.9 percent) of all the privately owned land in Brazil.

Also in accordance with the imperatives of the law promulgated in 1964, Brazil's Instituto de Reforma Agrária made use of a very complicated formula and classified the holdings into the following categories: minifundia; rural *empresas,* or farms on which the land is being used in an economic and rational manner in accordance with the economic possibilities of the region in which it is located and in accordance with norms established beforehand by the Executive Power; and two types of latifundia. On this basis over three-fourths (75.8 percent) of the landholdings in Brazil were classified as minifundia, only 2.4 percent as rationally conducted empresas, 21.8 percent as latifundia *"por exploração"* (i.e., the way in which the land was being used or unused), and only 279 (less than 0.1 percent) as latifundia on the basis of size alone. However, only 12.1 percent of the land was in minifundia, 4.7 percent in the empresas, 76.7 percent in deficiently used large properties, and 6.5 percent in the estates that were classified as latifundia solely on the basis of size.

To this starkly naked picture of the extent to which a few of the proprietors own and control the land, one must add the all-important detail that the bulk of the workers engaged in agriculture and pastoral activities are not farm owners or even tenants of any kind. They are landless agricultural laborers. The best estimates of this that I have been able to make indicate that three out of four of the Brazilian families that are dependent upon agriculture and stock raising for their livelihoods are headed by men who are not farm operators of any kind (owners, administrators, tenants, or even squatters) but are mere farm laborers dependent upon some kind of wage. This, of course, is merely one of the inevitable consequences of a system of *centrally managed* or administered large landed estates such as prevails in Brazil. (Quite a different picture holds in a country such as England, in which the large estate is divided for purposes of operation among a number of renters, each of whom is responsible for the management of his farm.) Clearly the Brazilian scene is one in which a few people own large amounts of land and enormous numbers of people possess little or none of it. This I consider to be the fundamental cause of the slowness with which the great agricultural potentialities of a huge half continent have been utilized. Until the ownership and control of the land is transferred to a far greater degree to those who actually work it, Brazil's agricultural development is sure to be far less rapid than desired and the level of living of the bulk of her rural population far lower than is necessary.

My basic reasons for believing this can be stated very simply. I cannot accept in any form the idea that cheap labor of any type, be it that of slaves, serfs, peons, or any other kind of servile or semiservile workers, is an acceptable status for any part of the human race. In short I reject completely the idea that any variety of a two-class system (made up of a small elite at one extreme and the huge mass of the manual laborers at the other, with few if any persons of intermediate status) is to be desired or even tolerated. Therefore, I am fully convinced that any society should shun, as it would the plague, a system of large landed estates, since they almost inevitably generate and perpetuate such a two-class social structure. In other words, after almost half a century of endeavor to understand rural societies of the past and present, I am fully convinced that the most important factor in the well-being of those who live from agricultural and pastoral activities in Brazil, or elsewhere, is the degree to which the ownership and control of the land is vested in those who work upon it on the one hand or concentrated in the hands of a few large landed proprietors on the other.

The germ of such a conclusion began to emerge in my mind when I was a boy in southern Colorado. There I could not fail to observe the contrasts between the way of life of those in several small communities of middle-class operators of family-sized farms and the extremes of wealth and poverty characteristic of most of those who spent their lives on the huge ranches in the surrounding areas. The unenviable conditions prevailed on the large estates even though they monopolized the highly desired land along the streams. This idea was reinforced when, in the 1930s, professional responsibilities made it important for me to attempt to understand and explain the reasons for the extreme differences of levels of health, education, safety of life and property, and other aspects of the levels of living in Louisiana and other parts of the Deep South. This came immediately after I had pursued studies of rural social organization leading to the Ph.D. degree in the corn and dairy belts of the United States, both characterized by a sociocultural system in which the ownership and control of the land was in the hands of the actual middle-class farmers. In Louisiana, as in neighboring Mississippi and Arkansas, and other southern states, I ran head on into the problem of "rich land, poor people." Here there was, for any who cared to see, undeniable evidence carefully assembled and analyzed by sociologists, economists, and home economists that the inhabitants of the unfertile, hilly sections of the region, where the farms were pitifully small, actually enjoyed substantially higher levels and standards of living than those of the rich, level lowlands where the members of the affluent planter class had installed their large cotton and sugar-cane plantations. As I searched for fuller comparative information about the effects of the large landed estate and the family-sized farm in other parts of the world and throughout history, every concrete case that could be brought under scrutiny made it clear that the effects of the two in the United States were by no means unique. Gradually I came to recognize that the history of mankind has been largely that of slavery and other forms of servile or semiservile labor—a situation due principally to the large landed estate and the sociocultural system it generates and perpetuates.

When, in the late 1930s, I had the opportunity of traveling widely throughout the Spanish-American countries, I already was fairly well prepared to anticipate what I would encounter in the vast rural areas extending from Mexico to Chile and Argentina, in which the hacienda system had dominated society for a period of four centuries, and as I visited hacienda after hacienda in Mexico, Peru, Chile, and the other countries, I found, in somewhat "enlarged prints," the same "two-class" system, a small handful of the elite and the masses of the people reduced to strictly lower-class socioeconomic status, that I had come to know far too well in the southern part of the

United States. Hence it is not strange that in 1942–43, when it was my good professional fortune to travel extensively through Brazil, I sought to make use of that exceptional opportunity and endeavored to observe and analyze the nature of the great sociocultural systems based upon extreme concentrations of the ownership and control of the widely distributed land. By this time, too, it was possible for me to follow some of the footsteps and verify the accuracy of the conclusions of such noted predecessors as Richard F. Burton. For example, in my travels in southern Minas Gerais, I too was able to see far below me the Paraibuna River as it "brawled down its apology for a bed," and to observe that the "houses and fields became more frequent, and the curse of the great proprietors is no longer upon the land." Moreover, although I was far less traveled and also otherwise less prepared than Burton had been, still I could share his thoughts about the social and economic influences of the large landholdings in Brazil. Clearly, "their effect is that which it has been in France, which was [and continues to be] in the Southern States of the Union, and which is in Great Britain. When will the political economist duly appreciate the benefit derived from the subdivision of the land!"[1]

As a result of this work, supplemented by observation in all parts of Colombia, and by a lengthy period of study in the Library of Congress, certain conclusions emerged. Therefore, when I published the first edition of *Brazil: People and Institutions* in 1946, I was prepared to state and defend the conclusion that "the size of the agricultural holdings, the concentration of landownership, or the distribution of landownership and control, is the most important single determinant of the welfare of people on the land."[2] Even then I had felt absolutely certain, theoretically and pragmatically, that in Brazil the concentration of the ownership of the land

... in the hands of a few and the reduction of the masses of the people to the position of landless agricultural laborers, is accompanied by: (1) a comparatively low average standard of living, although the elite landowning class may live in fantastic luxury; (2) great chasms of class distinctions between the favored few of the upper class and the masses who lack rights to the soil; (3) a comparative absence of vertical social mobility so that this chasm is perpetuated by caste barriers . . .; (4) a low average intelligence of the population because the high abilities and accomplishments of the few people of the upper class are greatly overweighed by the ignorance and illiteracy of the masses; and (5) a population skilled only in the performance under close supervision of a very limited number of manual tasks, and lacking completely in training and practice in managerial and entrepreneurial work.

After a quarter of a century of additional endeavor (in all parts of Brazil and in all of the other Latin American countries, in some of the world's major libraries, and in classes and seminars with graduate students working for advanced degrees), I believe I have gained an understanding of some of the salient features of the sociocultural system involved. The names of three of the principal varieties of this are the hacienda system, the fazenda system, and the plantation system. Common features of all are as follows:

1. Wherever large landed estates monopolize the land a two-class social structure is generated and perpetuated. This consists of a small number of the elite in a small, highly elevated socioeconomic stratum and a huge mass of landless agricultural workers at a near-servile level, if indeed they are not actually unfree.

2. Practically no vertical social mobility. The elite families are able to keep their own offspring in affluent circumstances, irrespective of their personal characteristics, and it is practically impossible for anyone to rise out of the lowly position occupied by the masses.

3. Very low average levels of intelligence (or ability to adapt to new situations) prevail, because most of the potentials of the masses of the people are unrealized.

4. Likewise when a system of large estates relegates the mass of the population to a creaturelike existence, the personalities of most people are sadly undeveloped. They acquire some skills in executing under rigid supervision a few manual tasks but never acquire the characteristics that feature saving and investment or those connected with the multifarious mental activities involved in decision-making and management.

5. Personal relationships between those who own and control the land and their representatives and those of the workers are of the order-and-obey type, that is, domination and subordination.

If space permitted, many other features of this sociocultural system could be identified and described, for in the highly integrated type of symbiosis involved, routine becomes all-important, manual labor comes to be considered degrading and demeaning, the average

standards and levels of living are very low, and there is little or no
incentive for most people to work and save. In fact, such a system
often means that the worker best serves his own interests by doing
everything possible to deceive the majordomo, overseer, or driver
into thinking he is exerting himself while actually doing just as little
as he can. It is hoped, though, that enough has been said to make
clear why I consider the system of large landed estates a dead weight
that Brazil must rid itself of before the bulk of its rural people can
ever attain the levels of living and the way of life to which they are
increasingly aspiring.

In conclusion, I desire to present brief quotations pertaining to the
socioeconomic effects of a system of large landed properties from
three of the most eminent sociologists who have ever lived, two of
them Brazilians and the other one of the founding fathers of American sociology. F. J. Oliveira Vianna, noted Brazilian lawyer-sociolo-
gist whose ancestors must have included at least one slave from
Africa, excellently summarized the idealist features (as seen from an
upper-class vantage point) of Brazil's huge landed estates as follows:

> ... we have been from the beginning a nation of latifundia;
> among us the history of the small farm can be said to go back
> only a century. All the long colonial period was one of the
> splendour of the immense landed estate. In this period it alone
> appeared and shined; it alone created and dominated; it is the
> central theme interwoven throughout the entire drama of our
> history for three hundred fecund and glorious years.[3]

At about the same time Edward A. Ross, one of the most widely
traveled and perceptive men of his day, who wrote dozens of books
about societies in all parts of the world, hit the nail exactly on the
head in his well-founded generalization about Brazil and other parts
of South America:

> Most travelers in South America have no eye for the fundamen-
> tals which make society there so different from our own. One
> may read a bushel of the books visitors have written on these
> countries without ever learning the momentous basic fact that
> *from the Rio Grande down the West Coast to Cape Horn, free
> agricultural labor as we know it does not exist.* In general, the
> laborers on the estates are at various stages of mitigation of the
> once universal slavery into which the native populations were
> crushed by the iron heel of the conquistador.[4]

And, finally, Gilberto Freyre, the most noted Brazilian sociologist, culture historian, and writer of our day, who himself had idealized the old-style sugar-cane plantation in Brazil, describes the situation currently prevailing on the modern plantations as follows:

In some areas, such as the sugar-cane plantation districts, the land serves only to provide what it can for industry, with the most archaic and anti-economic methods of production, by means of a poorly paid agrarian labour force and a rural population held as pariahs by the landowners. Not a few of these are absentees from the land which they have long owned and have little contact with their semiserfs, who live, it is well to repeat, in the condition of pariahs, while the urban workers and also the employees of the commercial establishments and banks and the public employees in the cities during recent decades have benefited from the legislation protecting labour and promoting social welfare. It was a situation in which the greater part of the rural population of Brazil was used on the rudest work on plantations and farms, on the estates of men with a mentality quite different from that which years ago characterized the relations between the landowners and their labourers, when the former were, most of them, a rural gentry: not only proprietors deeply attached to their estates but masters attentive to the needs of their workers in accordance with the patriarchal forms of association.[5]

9

Agricultural-Pastoral Conflict: A Major Obstacle in the Process of Rural Development

This paper posits the thesis that the age-old conflict between the agricultural and pastoral ways of life continues to be a major obstacle to agricultural and rural development throughout Latin America, and the same probably is true in many other of the so-called underdeveloped portions of the globe. A quarter of a century of professional involvement with Latin American societies has convinced me that improvement in the sociocultural system that is designated as "type of farming" is an indispensable part of the modernization of agriculture. I firmly believe that in most places it is of the utmost importance to combine both livestock and crop enterprises in a close symbiotic relationship in individual farm units. This definitely is not the case throughout Latin America, and this conclusion is exemplified by the fact that neither by personal observation, nor by reading, nor by questioning others have I been able to discover a single instance in which a farmer grows a crop of corn and then uses it to fatten his cattle for the market. In fact, Carl C. Taylor's observations in Argentina to the effect that corn is never employed in the fattening of beef cattle[1] apply equally well throughout all of the Latin American countries. Our contention is that the continued conflict between the agricultural and pastoral ways of life is a major factor in the persistence of inadequate types of farming.

In some of the more developed nations there are a number of excellent prototypes of the various combinations of crop and livestock enterprises that should serve as examples or models for those attempting to modernize the agriculture of Brazil, Colombia, Peru,

Reprinted from the *Journal of Inter-American Studies* 11, no. 1 (January, 1967): 16–43, by permission of the publisher, Sage Publications, Inc.

and many of the other countries of the Western Hemisphere. All of them involve the close symbiotic relationships referred to above, and all are examples of the well-rounded and highly productive agriculture that has produced high levels and standards of living for all those—the cultivators as well as the landowners—involved in agricultural affairs. Perhaps the dairy farms of northwestern Europe deserve first mention in this connection, especially those in Denmark in which the production of dairy products and the raising of bacon-producing hogs provide the economic bases for one of the most highly developed types of rural existence the world has ever known. The dairy farms of Wisconsin and other states in the dairy belt of the Great Lakes area of the United States may also be cited. Even more important in relation to Latin America, however, are the typical farms of the corn belt of the midwestern United States and the "rice–beef-cattle" farms of southwestern Louisiana. This is because the production of beef cattle, hogs, corn, and rice are and will continue to be among the most important enterprises carried on in the vast rural areas of Latin America. I believe that the corn–hog–beef-cattle combination of the corn belt deserves to be copied from Mexico to Argentina, and that a close intertwining of rice and beef-cattle enterprises would help solve most of the problems that hamper the production of rice on irrigated farms throughout Central and South America.

In order to keep the present paper in proper perspective, it probably is necessary to indicate explicitly that the particular sociocultural system designated as "type of farming" is only one of at least twelve large, intricate, and finely balanced complexes that make up the all-embracing social or societal system, or way of life, of any agricultural people.

Agricultural-Pastoral Conflict in the Cradles of Civilization

Of all the various expressions of social conflict in rural societies none has been more all-pervasive and enduring than that between rural sociocultural systems based upon the growing of crops and upon animal husbandry, respectively. All people who have received their religious heritages largely from Hebrew sources are well acquainted with the clash between the two as portrayed in the Old Testament, particularly in the story of Cain and Abel. The first

mention in Genesis of Adam's first-born son and the second is followed immediately with the information that the former was a tiller
of the soil and the latter a keeper of sheep. As far as we are told both
were equally conscientious in the performance of the prescribed
rituals for paying homage to Yahweh or Jehovah, one with a burnt
offering of the first fruits of his fields and the other with the finest
of the lambs in his flock. Moreover, as might be expected in a
chronicle derived from a pastoral people, the Lord was offended by
the smell of scorched grains and vegetables and gratified by the odors
given off by burned lamb. But to continue the story would necessitate
paraphrasing much of the Old Testament,[2] and logically it also
should be accompanied by the outline of the history of the Near East
and parts of the Mediterranean world from the time of Hammurabi
to the present.

Other important expressions of the chronic conflict between
agrarian and pastoral social systems in these cradles of civilization
are those involved in the endless struggles between the two large
segments of Arab societies, the nomadic Bedouin of the deserts and
the fellahin or peasants of the agricultural villages. Until very recently at least this seems to have been a dominant feature of society
throughout the Arab world, and perhaps no one has described better
the eternal conflict between the sedentary agricultural and the nomadic pastoral portions of Arabic societies than the noted French
sociologist Gustave Le Bon. This perceptive observer and incisive
analyst also described the type of accommodation through which by
paying a tribute of grains (from which the herdsmen could make
their bread) the agricultural villagers were afforded protection by a
specific group of nomads. Since apparently Le Bon's pragmatic study
of these Arabs has never been translated into English,[3] the following
is my own translation of a few of his most pertinent statements:

Thus the interests of the nomads and those of the sedentary
people are as diametrically opposed as those of the hunters and
the hunted, the former intent upon eating the latter, and the
latter engaged no less completely in trying to avoid serving as
food for the former. But since necessity is the most powerful
and eternal factor in the actions of human beings, an accommodation has been achieved rather easily, at least among the
Arabs, between these opposing interests. The villagers buy protection from the nomads by paying annual tribute, and the

latter protect the former so as to continue receiving the pay-
ments. It is true that the balancing of accounts is equivalent,
from the point of view of the sedentary people, to giving up a
part of the harvest in order to save the remainder; but in another form it is exactly what is done by the civilized man who
gives an insurance company a sum representing a part of his
harvest for the purpose of guaranteeing the same and gives the
government another part of the same harvest to help support
the officers of the law, the judges, and other civil employees who
have the responsibility for protecting him. Since the Arabs of
whom we are speaking have no government capable of main-
taining a police force and an army to suppress the raids, the
peasants prefer to pay off the marauders themselves, with the
results being identical and the expenses about the same.

On the other hand the tribute paid by the village Arabs to
the neighboring nomadic tribes makes the latter into allies who
must defend the peasants if other nomads attack them. But this
rarely happens because no tribe is anxious to get into war with
another, from which it would have little to gain, by attacking
a village that is under the protection of another tribe.[4]

Another of the most succinct and illuminating portrayals of the
conflict between the votaries of Pan and those of Ceres, however, and
one in which the barrier that had hampered agricultural development for thousands of years was finally resolved, deals with the
island of Cyprus. It was written by Sir Hugh Foot (now Lord Cara-
don), British colonial governor of the afflicted island. He succeeded
in dampening enough of the fires between the Greek and Turkish
factions that Cyprus could be granted independence. The following
paragraph contains a paradigm of what many of the "underdeveloped" parts of the world need most.

We tackled the age-old problem of the devastation caused by
the wandering herds of goats. These herds were owned and led
by tough, ruthless mountain goat-herds, who terrorised the
people of the settled villages and drove their goats through the
cultivation of the plains, destroying trees and crops as they went
and adding to the wide-spread damage caused by soil erosion.
We hit on the plan of appealing to the Greek love of politics.
We introduced a new law under which the people of any village

area could hold a local plebiscite. If the popular vote was in favour of the tethered goat, then the wandering herds of goats from the mountains would be outlawed. For some time no village dared to vote for the tethered goat. They feared the wrath of their traditional enemies, the mountain goat-herds. But then one village at last voted for the tethered goat. Immediately the full force of the police went into the area to enforce the decision. Within a month or two the result of the elimination of the damage done by the herds of goats began to be seen. One village after another applied for a goat plebiscite. Overwhelming popular opinion backed by the authority of the Government triumphed. A scourge for centuries past was brought under control, and in wide areas eliminated altogether.[5]

The Age-Old Conflict in Spain

Elsewhere throughout the Mediterranean world the traditional practice of transhumancy, or the seasonal movement of flocks and herds between the cool mountain pasturelands for summer grazing and the less rigorous climatic zones for wintering, supplied the ingredients for almost ceaseless conflicts between the farmers and gardeners and the herdsmen of one type or another. In no country, however, did transhumancy become more thoroughly embodied in the economy and nowhere were more privileges and immunities given to the potentates who owned and controlled the herds of sheep than in Spain. Consider in this connection a few brief extracts from the work of an English clergyman who perhaps was the most observant of the many visitors who have left us a record of the Spanish countryside.

> October 4 [1786], as we descended towards Leon, we overtook a Merino flock, belonging to the monastery of Guadalupe, in Estremadura. These monks have sufficient land near home to keep their flocks during the winter months; but in the summer, when their own mountains are scorched, they send their sheep into the north, where, having no lands, they are obliged to pay for pasturage. They were on their return towards the south.
> The great lords, and the religious houses to whom belong these transhumantes, or travelling flocks, have peculiar privi-

leges secured to them by a special code, called laws of the
Mesta; privileges, by many considered as inconsistent with the
general good.

This institution has been traced back to the year 1350, when
the plague, which ravished Europe for several years, had deso-
lated Spain, leaving only one-third of its former inhabitants to
cultivate the soil. But perhaps we ought to look for its origins
to more remote and distant ages . . . [p. 61].

The numbers of the Merino sheep are constantly varying.
Cajaleruela, who wrote A.D. 1627, complained that they were
reduced from seven millions to two millions and a half. Ustariz
reckoned in his time four millions; but now they are near five.
The proprietors are numerous, some having only three or four
thousand, while others have ten times that number. The Duke
of Infantado has forty thousand . . . [pp. 62–63].

When the sheep are travelling, they may feed freely on all the
wastes and commons; but, in passing through a cultivated country, they must be confined within their proper limits in a way
which is ninety varas [a vara is approximately one yard long]
wide . . .

In Spain, ever since 1350, . . . the laws of the Mesta have set
at variance the ploughman and the shepherd, prevented each
from deriving the least advantage from the other, insomuch
that five millions of sheep, under the sanction of a peculiar code,
not only fail to enrich the lands on which they feed, but effectu-
ally prevent its cultivation. Independent of the Merino flock,
many of the great landlords have suffered villages to go to ruin,
and have let their estates to graziers [p. 227].

. . . Farms, if inclosed, let much higher than those which are
open, because the latter are liable to be fed by Merino sheep;
whereas, should they enter the former, one-fifth of the number
trespassing would be forfeited. This, however, proved a never-
failing source of quarrels and contentions between the occupiers
of land and those who may be called graziers, that is, the
proprietors of the Merino flocks, who, under the sanction of a
peculiar code, claim the privilege of feeding, not only in the
common pasture, but even in plantations of olives. The murders
consequent on these quarrels have been more than two hundred
in the space of a few years; and the litigations have cost the
contending parties more than the value, both of their sheep and

of their olives. The council of Castille interfered, in the year 1570, to prohibit this; but the great sheep-masters plead their privilege, as granted by the Mesta code, and support their claim by force [pp. 284–85].[6]

For the present purpose of emphasizing the centuries-old conflict between pastoral and agricultural sectors of society that paralyzed Spain's agricultural development and undermined the foundations of the Spanish Empire, it is necessary to add only one brief paragraph from the pen of Gaspar Melchior de Jovellanos, one of the most noted Spanish intellectuals of all time. This brilliant social thinker, serving as mouthpiece for the Economic Society of Madrid in its appeal to the Crown through the Royal and Supreme Council of Castile for the promulgation of an Agrarian Law, closed his devastating analysis of the Mesta and its nefarious effects with the following words:

But if other people make use of transhumancy and protect the sheep lanes, none of them we know about have had and protected an organization of sheep owners united under the protection of a public magistrate in order to make war upon cultivated crops and non-migratory livestock, and ruining them through its privileges and exemptions. None of them permitted the enjoyment of various privileges of dubious origins, abusive in their application, pernicious in their objectives, and destructive of the rights of property. None of them established travelling tribunals in its favor and sent them into all parts [of their country] armed with an oppressive authority and as strong in subjecting the weak as they were weak in restraining the powerful. None of them legitimized its juntas, gave sanction to its laws, nor placed it in opposition to the defenders of the public. But enough of this. Society has discovered the evil: its assessment and suppression depend upon Your Highness.[7]

Pastoral Domination and Agricultural Subjection in Spanish America

The institutional complex called the Mesta never attained any great importance in the New World, although, as was almost inevitable, on paper its provisions were extended from the Peninsula to Spain's far-flung dominions.[8] Two reasons for its failure to flourish in the extensive area from what is now the state of California to Cape Horn are rather self-evident: (1) in most parts of America, cattle rather than sheep husbandry was the principal concern of the conquering Spaniards;[9] and (2) the Iberian overlords and their descendants did not need to use the provisions of its unjust code in order to maintain in subjection the Indian agriculturists, whom they quickly reduced to a state of vassalage. Nevertheless, the unceasing opposition of the indigenes, who lived by growing crops, to the large landed proprietors of European origin, who carried on a rudimentary type of cattle ranching on their extensive domains, has characterized the entire period from the sixteenth century to the present. Actual conflict between the powerful owners of the vast cattle haciendas and the weak and subjected agricultural masses, however, was most pronounced during two periods, namely, during the epoch of the conquest itself and during the struggle for agrarian reform that got well under way in Mexico about 1917 and swept throughout Latin America following the close of World War II.

In many respects the Spanish conquest of America featured the uprooting of the Indian populations from their established fields, which then were converted into pastures for the cattle and horses of the conquistadores, fully as much as it did the search for gold and the mines from which it could be extracted. As indicated in Chapter 6, the droves of swine of the agile "razorback" or "land pike" type (the only one known in European and American countries until well along in the nineteenth century) that served to a large extent as the commissaries for the expeditions of Benalcázar, DeSoto, and other explorers, were the spear points of the assaults by the Spaniards upon the Indians and their possessions in the New World. Very quickly they made dead letters of the numerous decrees, orders, and laws prepared by the Council of the Indies and promulgated by Spain's sovereigns that were designed to protect the lives and lands of the natives from the encroachments of the Europeans. Book Four (dealing with lands) and Book Six (devoted to the Indians) of the *Laws of the Indies* are replete with extracts from the regulations issued during the sixteenth and seventeenth centuries for the purpose of safeguarding the Indians and their fields from the greed and rapaciousness of the conquering stockmen. Nevertheless, the natives quickly were uprooted from their ancestral possessions and crowded back into out-of-the-way places and up onto the steep slopes of the mountainsides, frequently onto terrains so steep that they should never have been cultivated; and this left the rich, fertile, and well-located valleys for use as pastures for the livestock of the Spaniards.

The precise manner in which this was done, so that the officials could comply with the legal prescriptions that only vacant lands, that is, those not being used by the Indians, could be granted to the members of the expeditions, is indicated in some of the decrees in a way that leaves very little to the imagination. This procedure, inevitable perhaps when a powerful pastoral people equipped with firearms and horses imposed their overlordship upon hosts of poorly equipped peasant cultivators, is described rather fully in a decree promulgated by Charles V in 1550 that eventually became *Ley xii* of *Título XII* of *Libro Cuatro* of the code known as the *Laws of the Indies.* My translation of it is as follows:

> Because the estancias [ranches] of cattle, horses, swine, and other large and small animals, and especially those that are allowed to run loose, do great damage to the cornfields of the Indians: WE order that no estancias whatsoever be granted in places where such damage may result, and it is no excuse if they be at some distance from the villages and fields of the Indians, because for the livestock there are plenty of more remote lands and plants where they may be grazed without prejudice, and the justices shall provide that the owners of the livestock and those interested in the public welfare shall make use of as many herders and guards as may be necessary in order to prevent any damage, and in case some does take place they shall make satisfaction for it.

Hundreds of reports, travel accounts, and scientific treatises of one kind or another have called attention to the completeness with which the Indians were divested of their traditional land holdings by the Spaniards, but no one has coupled this with specific indications of the end result of the struggle between Spanish stockmen and Indian agriculturists better than Colombia's noted statesman Manuel Ancízar. In 1850 this perceptive observer, while serving as secretary for the famous Codazzi geological and geographical commission, repeatedly brought his mind to bear upon the matters in which we are interested at the moment. For example, in describing the forty miles of level road extending from Bogotá to Zipaquirá, over the rich dry bed of an ancient lake now known as the savanna of Bogotá, he recalled that it once was "the beautiful plain upon which the innocent Chibchas lived and worked."[10]

No small part of the waves of discontent, agitation, revolt, and revolution that have characterized the Latin American countries during the twentieth century, and especially since the close of World War II, is made up of direct and indirect expressions of the centuries-old conflict between the pastoral interests of the large landed proprietors and the pressing agricultural necessities of the lowly rural masses of the population. Among the most striking examples of this we may simply enumerate: (1) the central features of the Mexican Agrarian Revolution, which got under way about 1917 and which had as its fundamental objective the return to the villages of peasants the lands that had been incorporated into the predominantly pastoral haciendas; (2) the "invasions" of thousands of Peruvian haciendas by country people who claimed that portions of those estates had unjustly been taken from them, a widespread series of direct actions that as early as 1950 had already filled Peru's courts with about two thousand cases; (3) the forcible seizure by the actual cultivators of the lands of thousands of Bolivian haciendas, which immediately preceded Bolivia's agrarian reform of 1953; (4) the all-out and to date successful efforts of Argentina's large landowners, especially in the province of Buenos Aires, to block all proposed programs for agrarian reform in that richly endowed and pastorally dominated country; and (5) the intense agitation for agrarian reform programs throughout Latin America, and the considerable advances made in this respect in some of them such as Venezuela, Colombia, and Chile.[11]

Agricultural-Pastoral Conflict in the United States

Even in this brief treatment two major expressions of the conflict between the agricultural and pastoral ways of life in the United States require attention. One of these deeply affected the development process in the trans-Appalachian heartland of the nation from the late eighteenth century on for several decades, and the other is the chronic struggle between herdsmen and "sodbusters" on the western plains and in the Rocky Mountains, or the events that supply the themes for the grotesque caricatures of western life presently offered those who watch television programs or attend motion pictures at home and abroad. Each of these will be commented upon briefly.

Following the close of the French and Indian Wars (in the late 1760s), population began to filter across the Appalachian ranges and onto the headwaters of the Ohio, the Tennessee, and the Cumberland, with hunters in the vanguard. Soon, however, they were accompanied or followed by herdsmen, whose rangy cattle and fleet, long-limbed hogs roamed the woods on about the same basis as the "Indians' cattle," or the deer, bison, and other game. The farming activities of the early families along the cutting edge of the frontier were limited almost exclusively to the growing of small patches of potatoes and corn, especially the latter, from which they made their own bread and spirits. Gradually, as the game was decimated or frightened away, the pastoral activities of the pioneers waxed in importance and their hunting waned to some extent, although neither they nor their descendants for many generations lost their predilections for the hunt.

The opening of the Wilderness Road to wagon traffic in 1795 facilitated the movement of farmers into the areas west of the Alleghenies and thus contributed to the migration to Kentucky, Tennessee, Ohio, Indiana, Illinois, and Missouri by those groups that gradually came to contest the herdsmen's unchallenged monopoly of the land. After the opening of the Cumberland Road (built between 1811 and 1818) and the Erie Canal (1817–1825) the floodtide of new agricultural settlers encroached severely upon the domains previously enjoyed by the possessors of large numbers of half-wild cattle and hogs. Many of the stockraisers were crowded back into rough, hilly, out-of-the-way places, and others found temporary respite on the open prairies, for before John Deere perfected a plow (in 1837) that would scour when used on the rich soils of the heavily sodded plains, the unforested areas were anathema to the farmers.

Two brief quotations from one of the books written by Frank L. Owsley, who probably possessed the greatest mastery of southern history ever attained by one man, summarize the essentials of the process. What he has to say applies fully as well to Ohio and western Pennsylvania as it does to western Virginia, West Virginia, western North Carolina, eastern Tennessee, eastern Kentucky, and so on. According to this careful scholar:

By 1840 the better agricultural lands in the older states and in many parts of the newer ones had been sufficiently settled by farmers to interfere with grazing upon the open range, and the herdsmen had largely disappeared from such lands. Those who had not desired to settle as planters and farmers, but preferred their occupation and the frontier with its plentiful game, fresh cattle ranges, and scarcity of neighbors, took up their abode in the pine forests and in the mountains where other graziers had already settled because they preferred such country. Here, protected by the sterile, sandy soils of the piney woods and the rugged surface of the highlands, the herdsmen and hunters found sanctuary from the pursuing agricultural settlers. Thus it was agriculture rather than slavery that pressed these settlers into the less fertile and more rugged lands. This was an old phenomenon. From ancient times an agricultural economy has driven the livestock grazier into the deserts and mountains....[12]

In another paragraph Owsley attended specifically to the extension of the same basic struggle into the more western sections of our nation. Thus, after having reiterated that "it was agriculture, then, and not slavery—as has been said repeatedly in the discussion of the pastoral economy of the frontier—that drove the herdsmen from frontier to frontier and finally into the pine barrens, hills, and mountains," he stated explicitly: "After the Civil War this phenomenon was repeated when the farmers or nesters swarmed into the Great Plains and crowded the cattle ranchers farther and farther into the more arid regions."[13]

Hundreds of careful, reliable scholars have supplied details about the universality and intensity of the struggle between the ranchers and the farmers in the trans-Mississippi West. This erupted closely after the opening of the railroads and the "sport" of killing buffalo destroyed the basis of the livelihood of the Plains Indians and left the prairies relatively open to occupation by white settlers, and it continued until the entire area now known as the "corn belt" had passed quickly through a stage of wheat farming—a severe crisis occasioned by the opening of new wheat lands to the west and north of that belt —and had made the radical adjustment represented by the adoption and perfection of the corn–hog–beef-cattle type of farming. Few of the materials about the essential nature of the age-old conflict are more cogent, however, than the following extracts from a monograph by Edward O. Moe and Carl C. Taylor:

> Agriculture on the frontier, before the coming of the railroad, was languishing for the want of a market. Grains, such as corn and wheat, were impossible as market crops because of their bulk. Cattle of high specific value were saleable, and they provided their own transportation. Labor costs in caring for herds were small as was the capital investment under grazing conditions. These advantages of the cattle enterprise made Shelby County part of the cow country during the seventies, despite the railroads reaching Avoca in Pottawattamie County in 1869. The Shelby County papers took note of more than 800 head that were grazing in the county. Restraining laws, the spread of the practice of fencing, settlers using their enclosed land as wild-hay pasture, led to hostile encounters between farmers and graziers. Herders were warned about the trespassing of their herds. They were forced to seek open land farther West. There were few grazing areas in Shelby County after 1885.[14]

> Settlement to the east and south of Shelby County proceeded at a more rapid pace than within the county, leaving a relatively larger amount of open prairie here than elsewhere. Graziers sent their herds in relatively large numbers to pasture on this prairie. Even before 1870 a few small herds were being grazed in the county and the practice increased through the 70's and into the 80's. By the middle of the latter decade farmers definitely held the upper hand over the graziers and were able, with the help of more stringent restraining laws, to drive the graziers from the county.[15]

The Resolution of the Conflict: The Most Significant Example

Despite the near universality of the conflict between the agricultural and the pastoral ways of life, some parts of the world are noted for the thoroughly harmonious manner in which various types of animal husbandry and the production of one or more cultivated crops are combined in the same farm business. One of these is the dairy farming of northwestern Europe, and its transplantation by

English, Dutch, Scandinavian, and German colonists and immigrants to the United States. Denmark's dairy–bacon-hog type of farming is perhaps the highest expression of this.[16] A second, the rice–beef-cattle combination now prevailing on the old "second bottoms" of the Mississippi River in southwestern Louisiana is another. And a third, the corn–hog–beef-cattle type of farming that flourishes in the corn belt of the United States, or the great area once covered by luxuriant prairies and millions of head of American bison, a sociocultural region that extends from Ohio to eastern Kansas and Nebraska, the most significant area of all. The materials in this section deal only with the latter.

Space limitations preclude a presentation of an adequate "life history" of this fundamental type of farming, one that in many ways must be considered as the backbone of American agriculture and as the social and economic basis of the most satisfactory[17] rural way of life to be found in the United States. In other publications, however, I hope to document more fully the major propositions that appear in this section. Even at present, though, it is necessary to deal briefly with the essential nature of the corn–hog–beef-cattle type of farming, its origin and development, and the spread from its place of origin in eastern Ohio and Kentucky into the states of Indiana, Illinois, Missouri, Iowa, Minnesota, Kansas, Nebraska, and South Dakota.

Essential Nature of the System

The nature of the close symbiotic relationship between the three basic enterprises in the combination under consideration probably has never been expressed better than in the following paragraph:

> During the . . . early eighties, cattle began to be shipped in large numbers from the Western ranges into the corn-growing regions of eastern Kansas, Nebraska, Iowa, Missouri, and Illinois, to be fattened upon the corn crops. It was therefore in the heart of the corn country rather than in the range country that the packing houses were built for the slaughtering of animals and the curing of meat products. Kansas City, St. Joseph, Omaha, Chicago, and St. Louis became the great packing cities. *Owing to the practice of allowing hogs to fatten on the droppings*

of the corn-fed cattle, pork came to be, in a measure, a by-product of the beef-producing industry.[18]

In these succinct words one of Harvard University's most noted economists, himself born and reared on an Iowa farm and later the operator of a farm in California, sets forth the close interdependency on the farm in the corn belt between the growing of corn, the fattening of beef cattle, and the farrowing and fattening of hogs, and also indicated the relation of these to the location, growth, and development of some of the most important cities in the United States. Almost forty years after Carver summarized so brilliantly the essential nature of the most important type of farming in the United States, Carl C. Taylor specified in greater detail the nature of life and labor in the area where he himself was nurtured. One salient paragraph that shows the extent to which the crop and animal enterprises had been thoroughly adjusted to one another on the typical farm follows:

Although the area is best suited for, and primarily given over to, corn production, other crops are needed for animal feed and as factors in a crop-rotation system that is necessary to help maintain soil fertility. Corn-belt farmers therefore produce not only corn, but also oats, hay, soya beans, and some wheat; and raise not only hogs, but also an abundance of cattle, poultry, and some sheep. If what might be called an oat belt were to be located on a dot map, the map would be very similar to one of the corn belt; a beef-cattle map would include the heart of the corn belt; and a poultry map would show that the corn belt is one of the country's great poultry-producing areas. Fattened hogs and cattle are the easiest and most profitable mediums through which to market the cropland, meadow, and pasture products, but the whole farming process is far from simple. The care of a series of crops and of young and fattening animals, plus the care of buildings, fences, and machinery, distributes farm work over the whole year and makes corn-livestock farming a full-time occupation for all, or most, members of the farm family.[19]

Because a few exceptionally perceptive men such as Carver and Taylor noted and described the nature of the combination or system in the type of farming under consideration, one should not jump to the conclusion that this should have been apparent to and deemed significant by the majority of economists and sociologists who have studied the culture, economy, and society of the midwestern United States. Quite the opposite is the case. For example, the comprehensive and widely adopted textbook, *Farm Management,* by John D. Black, Marion Clawson, Charles R. Sayre, and Walter W. Wilcox[20] completely failed to consider the germ of the matter, even though they entitled one section as "Corn-Hog-Cattle Farms," and attended to specific problems the farmers using the system had to face, such as "buying feeders vs. raising" them, "alfalfa vs. corn silage," "hogs vs. cattle," "fattening calves vs. yearlings, vs. two-year olds," and "one vs. two litters per year."[21] Moreover, even in a few cases in which the authorities have recognized the nature of the symbiosis and understood the economic advantages of the combination, the explanations given of the origin and development of the system are completely erroneous. Consider in this connection the comprehensive work by Charles Wayland Towne and Edward Norris Wentworth entitled *Pigs: From Cave to Corn Belt.*[22] These authors did stress the importance of the combination of the three enterprises. The very first of the excellent illustrations used in their book shows Hereford cattle and Chester White hogs together in a pasture and carries the caption: "The base of corn-belt feed-lot profits—hogs following steers."[23] In addition they refer to studies made at the Iowa Agricultural Experiment Station which showed that "in 120 days of feeding, an average pig, following two steers, picked up the equivalent of 312 pounds of corn." They are completely in error, however, in attributing the use of this system solely to the "German" farmers of the corn belt and in implying that the practice arose out of the thrift of "the hardworking Teutonic husbandmen."[24]

The origin and spread of the corn–hog–beef-cattle type of farming necessitated the following three specific conditions and discoveries: (1) soils and climate favorable to the production of abundant crops of corn; (2) the discovery of great advantages to be derived from using corn for the fattening of beef cattle; and (3) observation of the fact that much of the corn that had passed through the bodies of the cattle was eagerly sought and utilized by pigs. Let us direct our attention, therefore, to the specific aspects of cultural development involved.

The Genesis of the Corn–Hog–Beef-Cattle Type of Farming

As is true in the cases of all large and complex sociocultural systems, the origin, development, and spread of this specific type of farming involved a long sequence of fortunate discoveries of new facts and combinations of previously existing cultural traits and complexes. If we are to understand why the corn–hog–beef-cattle type of farming originated in Ohio and Kentucky during the early part of the nineteenth century and never has been used in any other part of the world, we must consider the peculiar set of circumstances that prevailed in the Ohio Valley in the years from about 1800 to 1840.

Some of the most significant of these factors are the following: (1) this large area of rich soils was swept rather clean of earlier inhabitants and their cultural heritages by the westward surge of settlement; (2) those who participated in the transformation of the area from forests and heavily sodded prairies to open fields and pastures were land-hungry, venturesome, self-reliant men and women drawn from Virginia, Pennsylvania, and elsewhere from the original thirteen states and also from many of the countries of northwestern Europe; (3) the land system which the genius of Thomas Jefferson and his fellows designed for the public domain enabled genuine middle-class farm operators (persons equipped and prepared mentally and physically to perform all three of the economic functions, i.e., those of the proprietor, those of the manager, and those of the laborer) to obtain the ownership and control of relatively large tracts of land and to transform them into substantial family-sized farms; (4) the institution of slavery was excluded from the area to the north of the Ohio, and for this reason the plantation system with which it was associated in a Siamese-twin type of relationship likewise was unable to establish itself in Ohio, Indiana, Illinois, and the areas to the west of them, nor could any other form of servile or semiservile labor gain a foothold in the area; and (5) the diverse, heterogeneous cultural heritages carried by the families participating in the settlement process literally poured into the sociocultural crucible, wherein midwestern society was in the making, the most advanced knowledge and skills relating to the growing of crops and the raising of livestock possessed by the farmers of Europe and those of the settlers along the eastern seaboard of the United States.

Sociologists and anthropologists have demonstrated conclusively that cultural growth and advancement consist largely of fortunate combinations of previously existing cultural traits and complexes, and certainly the genesis, emergence, and growth of the type of farming we are discussing conform strictly to this rule. Therefore one should think twice before he dismisses the combination of enterprises under consideration as being of little or no consequence. My own belief is that this unique development gave the United States and the world the most highly perfected and satisfactory type of farming.

Indian corn, one of America's greatest contributions to civilization, is the central core of the type of farming under consideration. Although the Indians native to the area presently included within the United States never attained a maize culture comparable with that in Mexico, Central America, and what is now Colombia, in all of the English settlements from Georgia to Maine corn quickly became the principal breadstuff of those who colonized the present eastern seaboard of the United States. It also was used as a feed for livestock, although it soon was known that there were serious disadvantages to that practice unless farmers were willing to take the trouble to soak, to boil, or at least to grind the grain before giving it to their kine or swine.[25] Much of the corn that had not been soaked, boiled, or made into meal passed quickly through the bodies of the cattle and was wasted; and the hogs whose digestive systems for many thousands of years had evolved on diets of acorns, beechnuts, roots, and other soft foods were physiologically unable to deal with the hard, flinty grains of ripe maize. Even as late as 1849, according to reports secured from its correspondents in all parts of the nation by the predecessor of the U.S. Department of Agriculture, it was the general practice to boil or grind corn before feeding it to hogs.[26] As long as settlement remained east of the Appalachians, however, the use of corn as a feed for livestock was relatively unimportant, probably because yields were such that no large amounts of it could be spared for any purposes other than to meet the pressing needs for human food.

In the rich lands to the west of the mountains, though, the situation was quite different. Indeed, the prodigious quantities of maize that could be secured with a minimum of effort by Daniel Boone and his contemporaries quickly came to rival and then to excel the abundance of game and the lushness of the canebrakes as a magnet attracting hunter-herdsmen over the mountains and into the bluegrass districts of Kentucky, the Scioto Valley of Ohio, and other favorable locations on the frontier.[27] Owsley quotes a perspicuous paragraph from an account of the settlement of Blount County, Alabama, which accurately depicts the process in general:

> As they prepared to move into the wilderness, the prospective immigrants [sic] usually sent " . . . a few strong men, generally their sons, without families, deep into the then wilderness in the fall, to make corn and prepare for them. The father generally went with them and chose the place, and then went back to prepare for moving when the corn was made. A bushel of meal will suffice a man one month, and if he has no other than wild meat, he will require even less bread. In the fall season, place three or four men, one hundred miles in a wilderness, with proper tools and two horses, they will pack their bread stuff for the hundred miles—procure their meat—clear land—and produce corn sufficient to bread one hundred persons one year.[28]

Information pertaining to the role of corn in the settlement of the area north and west of the Ohio is equally explicit. For example, Clement L. Martzolff, who edited *The Autobiography of Thomas Ewing,* quotes from Walker's *History of Athens County, Ohio* the following highly cogent sentences, apparently words Ewing himself wrote early in the nineteenth century:

> . . . Sometimes the children were allowed, by way of picnic, to cut with the butcherknife from the fresh bear meat and venison their slices and stick, alternately, on a sharpened pit and roast before a fine hickory fire; this made a royal dish. Bears, deer, and raccoons remained in abundance until replaced by herds of swine. The great west would have been settled slowly without corn and hogs. A bushel of wheat will produce, at the end of ten months, fifteen or twenty bushels; a bushel of corn, at the end of five months, four hundred bushels, and it is used to much advantage for the last two months. Our horned cattle do not double in a year; hogs, in the same time, increase twenty fold. It was deemed almost sacrilege to kill a sheep, and I remember

well the first beef that I tasted. I thought it coarse and stringy compared with venison.[29]

Limitations of space do not allow us to follow further the fascinating story of the role of corn in the conquest of the continent, so attention is now directed to the second of the components, cattle grown and fattened for beef.

The half-wild cattle that herdsmen took across the Appalachians in the latter part of the eighteenth century and the opening decades of the nineteenth bore slight resemblance to the highly perfected Herefords, Angus, and other beef cattle of the present day, or even to the dual purpose shorthorns that enjoyed great popularity throughout the corn belt during the period from about 1850 to 1900. They were rangy, long-horned nondescripts that were similar in many respects to the ones that nightly are chased to the point of exhaustion on the television screens in the living rooms in millions of homes. Those that were taken from New England, New York, New Jersey, and Pennsylvania came from a system in which the bulls and steers were used largely for draft purposes, and the cows served to some extent as dairy cattle, although they too frequently doubled as work stock. After they became superannuated all were used for food. From Virginia to Georgia, cattle were raised primarily for beef, and most were driven on the hoof to northern markets, until the invention of the cotton gin and the burgeoning of cotton acreages forced the graziers to move their "cow-pens" to the western frontiers.

Early in the nineteenth century, in the new state of Ohio, there occurred the happy combination that solved for the great "farm belt" of the United States the conflict between the interests of the herdsman and those of the farmer and set the stage for the rise of the corn–hog–beef-cattle type of farming. The following paragraphs quoted from the 1850 issue of the *Report of the Commissioner of Patents* are pertinent:

> We are indebted to the Hon. J. L. Taylor, of Chillicothe, Ohio, for the following engraving and description of one of the best cows of the short-horn breed ever introduced into this country. The importation of short-horned cattle by the Ohio Company, and others, have effected a rapid improvement in the breeds and quality of the cattle in the Scioto valley, and great benefit has resulted, from their importation and sales, to that

section of the country. Due honor should be awarded to the enterprising capitalists through whose agency these results have been accomplished.

The Scioto Valley has become somewhat famous for the production of fine stock. From 25,000 to 30,000 head of the best fatted cattle annually driven to the Eastern markets, are taken from this valley, south of the National road. This great business, implicating the value of a million and a quarter of dollars, was commenced by the late Felix Renick, Esq., who was then a recent migrant from Hardy Co., Va. He and his brother George, in experimenting upon the virgin soils of this luxuriant region, then almost wilderness, found that immensely large crops of Indian corn could be raised with but little labor, but that there was no remunerating market for large crops of this staple within reach. They devised the project, thus for the first time conceived in this country, of fattening large herds of cattle with their luxuriant crops of maize, and *marching* their grain to distant marts in the shape of beef.[30]

The materials just quoted make it evident that the same enterprising men who hit upon the importance of feeding corn to beef cattle also were the ones who had much to do with the improvement of the types of cattle to which the grain was given. In fact, it was Felix Renick himself who helped organize the Ohio Company mentioned above and went as its agent to England, where he purchased a considerable number of the finest Durham cattle and made arrangements to ship them to the United States. That the dimensions of these activities were sufficient to have an important effect in improving the livestock used in the emerging new type of farming is evident from a story published in the *Sciota* [*sic*] *Gazette* and reprinted in the first volume of *The Farmer's Cabinet,* which began publication in Philadelphia in 1838. This story featured the "GREAT SALE OF DURHAM STOCK," imported by the Ohio Company during the years 1834, 1835, and 1836. The sale was held on October 28, 1836, at the Indian Creek Farm, the residence of Felix Renick, Esq., in Ross County. A total of forty-eight animals figured in the sales to buyers from eight counties in Ohio and from unspecified parts of Kentucky. Thirteen of the animals sold for $1,000 or more, with the top prices reported as being $1,505 for a bull named Comet Halley and $2,225 for a cow named Tees Water and her calf Cometess.[31] The outstanding cow mentioned in the preceding quotation, Violet, was owned by

George Renick and pictured in the *Report of the Commissioner of Patents,* but did not figure in this sale, as probably was the case with many other thoroughbreds imported during the early 1830s.

Much could be added concerning the improvements in cattle breeds and in the culture of corn—such as the fact that Henry Clay of Kentucky seems to have been the first or one of the first to introduce Herefords into this country[32]—but that would go far beyond our purposes here. Enough has been said to show rather definitely that the growing of corn and the fattening of specialized types of beef cattle early came to be tied together in ways that were highly beneficial to both farmers and consumers.

To conclude this discussion of how, in what is now the eastern extremity of the corn belt of the United States, the age-old conflict between the agricultural and pastoral ways of life was resolved and the corn–hog–beef-cattle type of farming generated, there remains the explanation of how the practice of having "the hogs following the steers" came into being. Probably we shall never know exactly when and where this important bit of farm management was hit upon, but surely it was in either the bluegrass section of Kentucky or the forested areas of eastern Ohio, or both, during the opening decades of the nineteenth century. It may have come as a result of including both hogs and beef cattle in the same herds of livestock that were driven from the areas west of the Appalachians to markets in New York, Philadelphia, and other cities.[33] Indeed, one leading authority on the history of the region has indicated that even the long, rangy hogs of that epoch had to be conditioned for journey by being run around in the fields for a number of days before they were started on the trip to the slaughter pens. He further states specifically the point in which we are most interested, that of tying the feeding of the hogs to the feeding of corn to beef cattle: "the loss of time resulting from a mixed drove of cattle and hogs was more than compensated for by the saving in feed, as the hogs could subsist on the undigested grain which fat cattle left."[34]

We also know that by about 1840 in Kentucky the best ways for organizing the practice had been reduced to a carefully planned system. In an essay "On Grazing and Feeding Cattle in Kentucky," which Adam Beatty included in his *Southern Agriculture, Being Essays on the Cultivation of Corn, Hemp, Tobacco, Wheat, Etc., and the Best Method of Renovating the Soil,* published in 1843,[35] we find the following instructions:

The cattle are to be kept on their respective grazing grounds until the 10th day of December. . . . When the grazing season is at an end, the cattle are to be carefully examined, and all those, which are intended to be butchered, the next year, are to be set apart for *full feeding,* and the residue are to be only *half fed.* Those that are to be *full fed* should be separated into lots, from fifty to one hundred each. . . . Each lot must have two *fields* to be fed upon, and the process of feeding will be as follows:

Each steer must have daily as much corn, fed with the fodder, as will be equal to half a bushel, shelled. . . .

There must be two fields for feeding each separate lot of cattle, and they should be fed alternately, day about, in each of these fields. When commencing in the morning, one load of corn should be hauled and distributed before the cattle are let in, so that they may be engaged in feeding, while the second load is distributing. . . .

When, on the next day, the cattle are removed to the second field for feeding, the hogs, which are to follow the cattle, must be turned into the field, in which the cattle were fed the day before. When the cattle are *full fed,* two hogs for each steer is the number that should follow the cattle . . . but only one hog to each steer should follow cattle which are to be only *half fed.* [36]

Obviously, the publication of such a detailed set of specifications for the express purpose of systematizing the practice means that the practice had originated at least a decade earlier.

The Spread of the Corn–Hog–Beef-Cattle Type of Farming

Only a few comments will be made concerning the spread of the combination of corn, beef cattle, and hog enterprises in the United States. Following its genesis early in the nineteenth century on the upper reaches of the Ohio and its tributaries, this sociocultural complex quickly took over as the typical type of farming throughout the entire area from eastern Ohio to eastern Kansas, Nebraska, and South Dakota. That is, it either accompanied wheat culture, or soon replaced it as settlement surged forward from the great forests of Ohio and Indiana and occupied the vast prairies westward. By 1880 it had replaced the buffalo and the Indians on the Great Plains as far as the 100th parallel. As a result, along with Ohio, the states of Indiana, Illinois, and Iowa, the northern half of Missouri, eastern Kansas and Nebraska, southern Minnesota, and southeastern South Dakota came to form the broad expanse in which sturdy, enterprising, middle-class farmers operating substantial family-sized farms made use of this ingenious sociocultural system. There are few other large areas in the world where the soil and climate are more favorable for the production of corn and livestock, and none in which mankind has rivaled the farmers of the corn belt in their ability to utilize those resources and their own natural endowments. To the north of the corn belt, in latitudes where corn did not find the hot, sultry nights that favor its growth, dairy farming gained undisputed sway; to the south, tobacco in Kentucky and the relatively poor and hilly lands in Missouri hampered the spread of this combination; and in western Kansas, Nebraska, and northern and western South Dakota the comparative lack of rainfall enabled the production of wheat to continue as the principal type of farming. Because of their proximity to the western ranges, portions of the area west of the Mississippi became those in which the finishing of beef cattle was of the greatest relative importance in the system.

The growing of crops, mainly wheat at first and then corn, could hardly have replaced free ranging cattle and hogs on the prairies had it not been for the perfection of a steel plow by John Deere in 1837,[37] and this was merely one step in the process by which the operators of family-sized farms, mostly in the midwestern United States, actually were responsible for the invention and perfection of a major share of all the modern agricultural implements and machines now available to assist man in extracting products from the soil.[38] These farmers also are the ones largely responsible for the improvement of corn varieties, the introduction and promotion of soy beans on the farms of the United States, the perfection of the lard types of hogs grown in this country, and even the development of the finest breeds of beef cattle. Furthermore, very recently they have brought about revolutionary practices in the feeding of both cattle and swine, a series of changes that very well may presage the dissolution of the tie between the fattening of beef cattle and the raising of pigs, that tie characterizing the sociocultural system we have been analyzing. But this aspect of the study must await additional data and form the basis for another essay.

For the present, the close symbiotic relationship between the growing of corn, the farrowing and fattening of swine, and the fattening of beef cattle still stands forth as by far the most important type of farming in the United States. It represents the solution on a large scale of the agricultural-pastoral conflict. And the combination involved offers a ready means whereby countries whose farmers already grow corn, raise pigs, and produce beef cattle may tremendously increase the production per man-year of their agricultural labor forces, the amounts of sadly needed proteins for the diets of their populations, and economically rewarding products for export.

Summary, Conclusions, and a Proposal

My major conclusions and their implications for the development process in the so-called developing countries can be stated very briefly:

1. The thesis is advanced that the age-old conflict between those who grow crops and herdsmen of various types is a major impediment to the process of development throughout Latin America and many of the other "developing" countries; the hypothesis is given that promotion of types of farming in which animal and crop enterprises are combined in a highly symbiotic manner within the same farming units offers a major opportunity to the nations and societies involved.

2. Illustrations are given of the almost eternal conflict between the cultivators and the herdsmen, beginning with the ancient Hebrews, passing to the Arab world, and then continuing with the tragic situation in Spain, the disastrous results when the pastoral interests of a handful of conquerors were superimposed upon the agricultural Indians throughout what now is Latin America, and the long-continued conflicts between the ranchers and other graziers on the one hand and the "sod-busters" on the other in the United States.

3. The origin, development, and spread of the corn–hog–beef-cattle type of farming, the one responsible for the highest average levels of living and general personality development on the part of farm people ever attained, is traced very briefly, and this type of farming is suggested as the key to solve the most acute and chronic

problems of underdevelopment in Latin American countries and others now in the "developing" stage.

4. Finally, in order to be very specific, the following comments are offered with respect to the proposed application in one given country, namely Ecuador. That delightful and interesting little country has about as good a claim as any other to the distinction of being the place of origin of Indian corn. Ecuador's humble campesinos know corn culture. They also have known and grown pigs from the earliest days of the conquest, for Benalcázar and his followers and his great commissary of hogs moved out of Quito in their endeavors to be the first to reach the Chibcha dominions on the savanna of Bogotá;[39] *lechón asado,* or roast suckling pig, is a national dish. And, in common with all of the other Spanish-American countries, the growing of cattle is the major economic interest of the powerful families who operate the country. In brief, all of the components of the sadly needed combination of farm enterprises already are tried and tested within the country itself, and, furthermore, all of the modern embellishments such as hybrid varieties of corn, effective pesticides, up-to-date techniques for slaughtering and preserving the meats, and so on, can easily be added, for these are parts of the total requirements that various specialists and agencies are ready and avid to supply and promote. All that is lacking is the proper combination of the enterprises.

But (and this is the reason for devoting these concluding remarks to Ecuador, rather than to Colombia, or Venezuela, or Peru, or one of the others) an elaborate set of recommendations for the development of Ecuador's agriculture has just been released in a report of the Inter-American Committee on Agricultural Development, which has its seat in the Pan American Union in Washington, D.C. These recommendations assign corn twenty-first priority, third from last in a list of twenty-three products (outranking only potatoes and cotton), in a descending order in which barley and wheat occupy the eleventh and twelfth places, respectively, and in which the top three are bananas, fibers other than cotton, and legumes, in the order named. Moreover, the experts preparing this report recommend that the acreage planted to corn be reduced from the 227,000 hectares planted in 1963 to 208,000 hectares in 1968 and to 199,000 hectares, in 1973. They do "program," however, an increase in production (not in itself impossible), from 164,000 tons in 1963 to 300,000 tons in 1973.[40]

My recommendations would be that the acreage devoted to the production of corn be maintained and increased, that this golden grain (golden frequently in color and always in the economic sense) be given the highest priority, and that every effort be made to install and foster a genuine corn–hog–beef-cattle type of farming in Ecuador. If necessary, and it probably would be necessary, the device used by Seaman A. Knapp first on the prairies of Louisiana and later throughout the South—the initial steps which eventually grew and developed into the United States Agricultural Extension Service—should be used. This was the employment of experienced farmers to organize and operate farms on which the growing of crops and the animal husbandry enterprises were all integrally combined in the same farm business units.[41] Knapp, who had cajoled grain farmers in Iowa, where he was a swine breeder, founder and publisher of the journal that eventually became *Wallace's Farmer,* and later president of Iowa State College, had to hire ex-grain farmers from the Midwest to operate farms in Louisiana in accordance with his instructions. Only then was he able to bring about a combination of livestock and crop enterprises on the grassy plains that were previously considered absolutely useless for anything other than a rudimentary pastoral economy. The fact that quite by accident a few of these ex-wheat farmers discovered that they could apply their customary horse power, machines, and methods to the growing of rice was a rich premium that quickly gave rise to a unique, new sociocultural complex, the rice–beef-cattle type of farming that now prevails in by far the most prosperous section of Louisiana.

Finally, there are, in addition to Ecuador (especially the broad coastal plains of that country) many other portions of Latin America in which high priority in agricultural programs should be given to bring about a closely integrated type of farming in which the growing of corn, the fattening of beef cattle, and the raising and fattening of pigs and hogs are the basic enterprises. These include portions of the plains at the eastern and southern bases of the Andes Mountains in Colombia and Venezuela; the upper portions of the Sinu Valley in Colombia and much of the plains of Bolívar in the same country; the corn belt of Argentina and other extensive parts of that nation's great pampa; the area about Barretos in northwestern São Paulo, Brazil; the "Triangulo" area of Minas Gerais, Brazil; the Papaloapan Valley of Mexico; the Pacific coastal plain in Nicaragua; and the Nicosia Peninsula in Costa Rica.

PART V

On the Positive Side

Although the obstacles to rapid increases of food, feed, and fiber in Latin America are tremendous, and only the overcoming of those obstacles will enable agricultural production to keep pace with or outdistance the rapid growth of population in the area, the situation is not entirely bleak. Two selections from *Brazil: People and Institutions* are presented on the roles of the spread of new settlement and a remarkable rise of dairying, respectively, in increased production to illustrate why per capita consumption in Brazil actually has been rising. Finally, an analysis and description of the role of improved ways of farming was prepared for inclusion in this concluding part of the book.

10

The Surge of New Settlement in Brazil

Although the din of the debates and the plethora of projects for agrarian reform since 1960, which are discussed below, resulted in relatively little colonization in the sense of planned subdivisions into farms of large landed estates, spontaneous movements into and settlement or thicker settlement of many areas have contributed greatly to Brazil's ability to feed her own people and to export farm products to other countries. Moreover, in the 1970s and especially in connection with the building of the Transamazonian Highway and other road projects, the national government once more is engaged in organized colonization projects on a large scale.

Since 1920 the rapid expansion of settlement into previously heavily forested areas was by far the most important factor in Brazil's increased production of the means of subsistence and the commodities she has put into the streams of international trade. Of all of this, the phenomenal conquest of a large part of the state of São Paulo for agricultural purposes was the most spectacular and important. It is important to keep in mind that during the 1950s and the 1960s, the spread of São Paulo's established system of coffee culture into northern Paraná constitutes one of the outstanding chapters in Brazil's entire agricultural development. In fact, by 1968 Paraná was producing almost half the coffee grown in Brazil, or 1,004,000 tons of the national total of 2,115,000 tons and almost double the 552,000 tons credited to São Paulo.[1] Other outstanding features of the conquest of previously almost unused sections of Brazil during the 1960s are

From T. Lynn Smith, *Brazil: People and Institutions,* 4th edition (Baton Rouge: Louisiana State University Press, 1972), pp. 645–51. Reproduced with the permission of the Louisiana State University Press.

the settlement of large areas of the Rio Doce Valley in Minas Gerais, the opening of the rich new lands in central Goiás, and the heavy onslaught by migrants from the Northeast (using their primitive and destructive system of fire agriculture) upon the forests of northcentral Maranhão. In both Goiás and Maranhão the expansion of rice culture, accompanied by that of subsistence crops such as beans and manioc, is the principal enterprise of the new settlers. In fact by 1968 Goiás, with an estimated production of 1,250,000 tons of rice (up from 724,000 in 1960), was on the verge of replacing Rio Grande do Sul, with 1,286,000 tons, as the largest producer of this great staple in the Brazilian diet; and Maranhão, for which the estimated production in 1960 was only 278,000 tons, had increased its total to 740,000 tons in 1968, when it was exceeded in this basic activity by only Rio Grande do Sul, Goiás, Minas Gerais (1,039,000 tons), and São Paulo (815,000 tons).[2] These data, and others that might be supplied about the great expanded production of the corn, beans, manioc, and other crops on which the settlers depend to feed their own families, should demonstrate conclusively that the spontaneous settlement of virgin lands has contributed substantially to the increased production of food in Brazil.

In the early 1970s Brazil's government again undertook large-scale efforts to colonize extensive areas of the public domain, especially in connection with the construction of the Transamazonian Highway and other roads in the immense, almost uninhabited portions of the national territory. One probably is not far wrong if he thinks that this is intimately related to some of the "spin off" or side effects of the construction during the 1960s of the Belém to Brasília highway, for much spontaneous settlement radiated from the hundreds of villages and towns that sprang up along the lengthy and badly needed truck route. For example, as has been indicated in Chapter 2, one analyst, after describing the enormous increases in the production of rice, manioc, beans, and corn in Maranhão since the late 1950s indicates that

... the tonic that led to this development was the opening of BR-10, Belém-Brasília, at the beginning of the decade. For example, the city of Imperatriz—[in the município] which produces the finest rice in Maranhão—experienced an increase of 67 per cent in recent years, and presently is estimated to have 42,000 inhabitants. ... The opening of new roads is the most important development. According to a report by the Conselho Nacional de Economia, the increase in the production of babassú and rice is due to the opening of new roads, which permit the establishment of new colonies, and form new fronts of agricultural production.[3]

It also seems certain that the remarkable growth and development of the city and município of Ceres, Goiás, which was started in the 1940s as the Colonia Agrícola de Goías, played a part in convincing Brazil's leaders that it was high time to renew the planned settlement projects in the agricultural development of the nation. In any case, with great fanfare, in 1970 the Brazilian government launched the greatest road-building and colonization program in Brazil's history. The kickoff came on March 18, 1970, when "the President of the Republic announced that actual work on the Highway System for the Colonization and Integration of the Amazon, to be developed by 1974, was to begin immediately, having as its basic component the Belém-Brasília Highway." He then announced:

> During the current year the paving of the stretch Anápolis-Jaraguá-Ceres will be completed, and this will be followed by the paving of the stretch from Ceres to Porangatu, already included in the financial negotiations with the World Bank.
>
> Of equal importance with the Belém-Brasília in the opening of the Amazon is the linking of Cuiabá and Pôrto Velho, which also recently has been assured, permitting regularity of transportation by road to the capital of Rondônia, from whence the work will proceed so as to reach this year Rio Branco [Acre] and the Brazilian-Peruvian boundary.
>
> Work also will go ahead in the construction of the road that will link the capital of Amazonas [Manaus] and South-Central Brazil, by way of Pôrto Velho and Cuiabá—with the completion of the stretch from Manaus to Pôrto Velho also planned for this year.
>
> Related projects also are being developed by the Ministry of the Army and the Ministry of Transportation . . . for the completion of the road that will link Manaus with Caracaraí and Boa Vista, and extending to the boundaries with Venezuela and Guiana and of the highway that will connect São Luís and Teresina and Belém, which also is scheduled for completion this

year.

Coordinated with the work undertaken in connection with
the projects just mentioned, this third government of the Revolution will amplify its contribution by undertaking two new
fronts in the building of the basic road system of Amazonia.
The first consists of the construction of a highway of penetra-
tion along the longitudinal axis of the region, uniting Cuiabá,
Cachimbo, Coração de Selva, and Santarém, a port on the
Amazon River. This road will function as a truly new route for
the movement from south to the north, making use of the
alternative system of the Cachimbo region. The second will
consist of the construction of a pioneer highway uniting the
Northeast and Amazonia. Starting with the terminuses of the
roads in the Northeast's system, this highway will cross the
Belém-Brasília at Marabá on the Tocantins River, and follow
across the valleys of the Xingu and Tapajós rivers to Humaitá
where it will form a junction with the Pôrto Velho-Manaus
highway.

With an extension of 6,750 kilometers [about 4,200 miles],
this road, which may be called the Transamazonian, will link
the terminal points of navigation on the southern tributaries of
the Amazon and will be a clear pathway for the northeasterners
in the colonization of the enormous demographic vacuum and
the beginning of the utilization of the hitherto inaccessible
potentialities of the area.[4]

Less than eight months after this momentous announcement, the
president, on October 9, 1970, went to Altamira, Pará, where he
"watched the felling of a tree of more than fifty meters height,
symbolizing the overcoming of one more obstacle in the construction
of the road. This solemnity marked the initiation of work on the
construction of the Transamazonian Highway."[5] The first work was
on the vast portion in the state of Pará. A few months later, on
January 11, 1971, "contracts were signed for the construction of the
second part of the Transamazonian Highway, between Itaituba and
Humaitá, in the state of Amazonas, an extension of 1,000 kilometers."[6]

Some of the details of the grandiose plans for colonization in the
monumental endeavors to conquer and settle the Amazon were published in August 1970.[7] The authorization for the vast undertaking

Map Showing the Route of the Transamazonian Highway and Other Highways of National Integration (Courtesy Brazilian Embassy, Washington, D.C.).

is Decree-Law No. 1,106, which established the Program of National Integration. The territory to be included consists of the areas in which two existing agencies, or the superintendencies for the development of the Northeast and the Amazon, respectively, already were working. In the Northeast the promotion of irrigation projects is the chief type of development envisaged, and in the Amazon road building and colonization are major facets in the program. (In passing I cannot help but express the hope that sooner or later those in charge of SUDENE, the agency for the Northeast, will do what is necessary to promote the growing of alfalfa and its transformation into meat and milk in that potentially great but constantly bedeviled region.)

The law itself specifies that "there shall be reserved for colonization and agrarian reform the band of territory 10 kilometers deep on each side of the new highway, so that, with the resources of the Program of National Integration, the occupation of the land and the adequate and productive utilization of the same will be accomplished." This same decree assigned the Ministry of Agriculture the responsibility in the Amazon for "colonization and agrarian reform by means of planning and conducting studies and the establishment of projects for the development of agriculture and animal husbandry and the processing of farm products, including the necessary expropriations of land; the selection, training, transportation, and settlement of colonists; the organization of urban and rural communities, and the provision of the basic services required in each."

In his announcement of the plans, the minister of agriculture stressed that the new settlements were to be carefully planned and directed and not allowed to develop merely in a spontaneous manner. Specifically, he declared that "the granting of lands—at nominal prices and within the reach of any family—will be carried on as the road is built. Making reference to what occurred in the building of the Belém-Brasília Highway [he stated]: at the conclusion of this project, which lacked the planning of the Transamazonian, there already were 600,000 persons living in reasonably comfortable circumstances on the lands adjacent to it." Finally, he indicated that, to begin with, each family of colonists would receive an allotment of land fronting on the highway for a distance of from 200 to 250 meters and extending to a depth of 10 kilometers. This means that the holdings will vary in size from about 500 to 625 acres. One-half of each allotment is to be maintained in forest.

Inasmuch as the great Amazonian Basin (which includes not only an immense portion of Brazil but huge expanses of territory in Venezuela, Colombia, Ecuador, and Bolivia as well) forms the one great and potentially fruitful part of the world remaining to experience the impact of twentieth-century sociocultural influences, the present endeavors of the Brazilians are of the utmost interest. Moreover, those who get best acquainted with the immense area are prone to exude the kind of optimism about its possibilities that was exhibited a century ago by some of the world's greatest naturalists, who spent many years observing plant and animal life throughout the vast reaches of its virtually unpopulated area. I myself have reacted to many areas in Brazil (and also in Colombia, Peru, and Venezuela) as did Alfred Russell Wallace, coarchitect with Darwin of the theory of evolution.[8] (See also Chapter 12, pages 163–64.) It is true that my own view of the potentialities and especially the difficulties is influenced strongly by some knowledge of the experiences of the colonies of Confederate exiles from the United States.[9] It also is tempered by an appreciation of a few of the sociocultural and political obstacles involved. Nevertheless, as indicated in Chapter 5, I continue to think that the building of the Transamazonian Highway and the other roads already projected, and the construction of a "bee-line" modern highway to link Villavencio, Colombia, and Caracas, Venezuela, could mean fully as much for the agricultural, industrial, and commercial development of the northern part of South America as the Aswan Dam will for northern Egypt.

11

The Phenomenal Development of Dairying in Brazil

The term *type of farming* denotes, of course, a given combination of enterprises or the exclusive use of only one enterprise in any agricultural or pastoral entity logically entitled to be classified as a farm. Thus the type of monoculture so roundly denounced by Gilberto Freyre and dozens of other Brazilian thinkers—the sugar *engenho* or *usina,* the coffee fazenda, and even the extensive cattle fazenda—typifies traditional Brazilian types of farming that for the most part involve a single enterprise on a given farm. However, plantations on which the production of rice is combined with the growing of beef cattle or the planting of corn is combined with the farrowing and fattening of hogs (long important in the small farming areas of Rio Grande do Sul) are other distinctive types of farming. By all odds the type of farming that has done most to increase and add to the variety and adequacy of Brazil's food supply is the polyculture, involving the production of fresh vegetables and fruits, which was brought to Brazil by the two hundred thousand Japanese immigrants who settled in São Paulo and a few other states during the 1930s. During the 1970s there is every reason to suppose that this highly productive type of farming will be extended to many other sections where changing eating habits in rapidly growing cities and towns demand fresh fruits and vegetables.

Perhaps the most significant of all the changes in types of farming now taking place in Brazil, however, is (at long last) a rapid improvement in and expansion of dairy husbandry. To one born and reared

From T. Lynn Smith, *Brazil: People and Institutions,* 4th edition (Baton Rouge: Louisiana State University Press, 1972), pp. 665–75. Reproduced by permission of the Louisiana State University Press.

in an area where the people knew how to secure dairy products and how to use them effectively for the nourishment of large families, the almost complete lack of milk and milk products in most parts of Brazil was one of the greatest "cultural shocks" experienced when I first began to learn about Brazil and the Brazilians in 1939 and the early 1940s. This was emphasized when in 1942–43, while my family was living in Rio de Janeiro, milk of some kind was needed for our two small children. We were not even sure that lengthy boiling would make it safe for them to drink in those years. Subsequently, as I delved into the study of the origins and dissemination of this specific sociocultural system, I came to realize that real dairy husbandry was an achievement of peoples of northwestern Europe, and that only those cultures transplanted from that area would know much about the production of milk and milk products and integrate them as fundamental parts of their diets.[1]

All during the period 1942–51 when I traveled extensively throughout Brazil, anything related to dairying was so seldom encountered that I usually made a note of it in my diary, and extracts from that diary constitute large portions of the first two editions of this book (*Brazil: People and Institutions*). Most of those rare entries[2] concerned developments on ultramodern fazendas, the once-a-year visits during calving time of proprietors to their cattle fazendas, the milking of Zebú or Brahma cows giving about a quart per day, and dairy husbandry in the German settlements in south Brazil. In fact, the more I traveled throughout Brazil the more I became convinced of the validity and importance of Gilberto Freyre's generalization that "however strange it may seem the table of our colonial aristocracy [who resided on great plantations] was lacking in fresh vegetables, fresh meat, and milk. . . ."[3] Moreover, I became thoroughly convinced that the role of milk in Brazilian dietary practice had not changed radically from colonial days to the 1940s.

In the 1940s and more so the 1950s, however, dairy husbandry and the consumption of milk in Brazil began to take on new aspects. One of the important happenings was the initiation of measures by the national and state governments to insure the safety of those drinking milk. In my diary, for example, is an account of a visit in 1942 to a small coffee fazenda near Marília, São Paulo, where "in addition to coffee, some cotton is grown in the lowlands, and there are 20 head of milk cows. Others were sold yesterday. There is a new requirement that all milk must be pasteurized, and the processing plant pays only 2½ cents per liter. This is unsatisfactory so they have sold all the cows except those needed to supply milk for them and their colonos, of whom there are about 20 families." With the publication of the 1952 issue, the *Anuário Estatístico do Brasil* began giving some data on the production of milk in Brazil. The first figures, going back to 1949, are for pasteurized milk, and the totals reported are 149,999 and 161,460 metric tons[4] for 1949 and 1950, respectively. Of the total, about 60 percent was produced in Minas Gerais and 35 percent in the state of Rio de Janeiro. São Paulo, third in production, reported only 9,671,000 liters (5.6 percent), and the only other states figuring in the list were Espírito Santo and Santa Catarina.[5] Thereafter, both the production and the data about the same increased rapidly. In 1960 the reported production of pasteurized milk had risen to 363,955 metric tons, or 125 percent above the 1950 total, and the list of states in which pasteurized milk was produced had been expanded by the addition of Guanabara and Paraná. By 1960, moreover, São Paulo rapidly was getting into the picture of milk production. By then it accounted for 13 percent of the volume of the pasteurized milk, and largely as a result of this, the proportions for Minas Gerais and the state of Rio de Janeiro decreased to 49 and 33 percent, respectively. By 1960 figures also became available for the production of fresh milk in general, and this amounted to 4,899,816 metric tons. Of this, 33 percent was attributed to Minas Gerais, 25 percent to São Paulo, 8 percent to Rio Grande do Sul, 7 percent to Goiás, and 6 percent to the state of Rio de Janeiro.[6]

During the 1960s Brazil took gigantic strides to improve the quality and increase the amounts of milk and milk products available to figure in the diet of its rapidly growing population. By 1970 it ranked among the important milk producing countries of the world, a position that is certain to improve greatly during the 1970s. Indeed, according to a report by the agricultural attaché at the American Embassy in Rio de Janeiro, by 1968 milk had come to rank fifth in value among all Brazilian farm products. At this time its estimated value ($536 million) was exceeded only by those of beef ($986 million), coffee ($686 million), corn ($575 million), and rice ($551 million), and it was well ahead of the other five in the list of the ten most important agricultural products, that is, cotton (lint and seed combined), sugar cane, pork, bananas, and dry beans, in the order named.[7] This new high rank of milk in the list of Brazil's ten most valuable farm products came only after the spectacular increase in dairy husbandry that took place in the 1950s was followed by additional great gains in the 1960s. Specifically, the data given in the 1962 and the 1969 issues of the *Anuário Estatístico do Brasil* show that between 1960 and 1968 the production of milk rose by 2,124,633 metric tons (or 45.2 percent) and that of pasteurized milk by 135,638 metric tons (or 37.3 percent).

Little if any analysis has been made of the factors that are responsible for the recent rapid expansion of dairy husbandry in Brazil, although from the theoretical as well as the practical standpoints few subjects offer greater challenges or rewards to the serious student of sociocultural change than this sharp break with long-entrenched ways of life. Moreover, at least a few of the more significant of the factors may be identified rather easily. Years ago Carlos Borges Schmidt, one of the most perceptive sociologists who ever lived and worked in Brazil, observed and described in some detail the "invasion" of the mountainous sections of eastern São Paulo by cattlemen from southern Minas Gerais. Consider a few of his portentous statements.

> After having been invaded and dominated [for about a century] by the culture of coffee the Paraíba Valley underwent a second invasion. Cattle growers from the state of Minas Gerais established themselves in Cruzeiro and subsequently pushed up the river. In a short time the lands of the Paraíba Valley, previously abandoned, were occupied in a large part by the herds. To penetrate the Paraitinga Valley and that of the Parabuna was only a step.
>
> This stock raising on the extensive scale necessitated great areas of territory. Land was relatively cheap, in comparison with the prices prevailing in the state of Minas Gerais. It cost little for the *mineiro* cattlemen to occupy an ample area of ground. . . . It is not difficult to comprehend the disorder introduced into the agriculture of the region with the entrance of the *mineiros* who acquired the best land. A zone that had been essentially agricultural saw itself day by day being transformed into a pastoral region. The newcomers acquired parts of the old *fazendas* and turned in their cattle. . . .
>
> Throughout the entire valley of the Paraitinga agricultural production fell to the lowest level on record. Until a few years

ago São Luís was considered the granary of Taubaté. . . . [Now]
the situation is reversed. . . .

As a result the open country is abandoned. The inhabitants
of the rural zone move into the small urban center. Finding no
employment there, they make their way to the larger cities.[8]

Then came the great transformation. As described by Schmidt,
who knew the region intimately and spent all the time he could
studying the life and labor of its people:

About ten years ago [i.e., about 1940] a small truck, already
much used and well-worn, initiated a revolution in the economic system in São Luís. Early each morning this pioneer
truck left the city en route to Taubaté, picking up along a route
of 50 kilometers all the milk which the cattle growers had
brought out to the side of the road.

When cattle raising was established in the region, the cattlemen limited themselves to cattle breeding proper. [They had
herds of Zebú or Brahma cattle.] They milked very little, some
of them merely enough for domestic needs. Others made a little
cheese. . . . Scattered over a relatively large area, lacking easy
means of transportation, they had no way of undertaking profit-
ably the production of milk, since this product deteriorated so
rapidly. But one cattle grower with greater economic resources
resolved to initiate a new enterprise. He made arrangements
with the milk cooperative in Taubaté, entered into contracts
with various other cattle owners, and assumed the responsibility for the initial expenses.

For a long while that truck left São Luís in the morning and
reached Taubaté about noon, when it delivered to the cooperative the milk picked up along the way. At first there was very
little—200, later on 500, and then 600 liters of milk over the
entire distance.

The milk was sold to the Taubaté cooperative and a certain
amount charged to pay the cost of transportation. The remainder which the stockmen came to receive monthly served as a
stimulus to give a new orientation to their methods of cattle
raising. Instead of being interested merely in cows to raise
calves, they came to give some preference to those that would
produce some milk as well. As a result the production of milk

increased considerably. It was not many years before São Luís had become, in turn, an important milk center. [In 1950 it has] a plant which receives all the milk from those portions of the *município* which are served by roads. From Catuçava, which is 18 kilometers in the direction of Ubatuba, and from Lagoinha, 24 kilometers in the direction of Cunha, two trucks daily collect over 4,000 liters of milk which is made into cheese and butter in the local factory. The livestock industry is expanding and taking in new areas. In place of corn and beans, in place of sugar cane—made into *aguardente* and *rapadura*—in place of tobacco and rice, São Luís has come to produce milk and calves.[9]

Give or take a few years, the change described by Schmidt in the valley of the Paraitinga he knew so well also took place in immense areas of southern and eastern Minas Gerais, much of the state of Rio de Janeiro, parts of Espírito Santo, and eastern São Paulo, all of which presently are in the huge "milk sheds" of Brazil's two immense metropolitan centers.[10]

Once the stage had been set by the push of cattlemen from the north into the old decadent coffee plantation areas of the mountainous areas of heavy rainfall in the southern part of Minas Gerais and throughout the areas drained by the Paraíba River and its affluents in the state of Rio de Janeiro and eastern São Paulo, progress in the development of dairy husbandry in the zones near the great cities of Rio de Janeiro and São Paulo moved quickly. As already indicated some of the more enterprising herdsmen began taking a quart or so of milk per day from their rangy cattle of Indian origin (Brahma or Zebú breeds) and getting it to the milk-processing plants that sprang up in major towns and cities. As the area urbanized by leaps and bounds, the demand for milk rose dramatically. Thereafter the extent to which Brazilian farm operators adopted and put into practice a few of the other features that characterize modern dairy husbandry (as practiced in countries such as Denmark, the Netherlands, and the Great Lakes region of Canada and the United States) marked the speed with which the production and consumption of milk increased in the most densely populated sections of Brazil. Among these features are: (1) the upgrading of the livestock, substituting cattle selected and bred for their milking qualities for the rangy beef types previously the rule; (2) the improvement of pastures, first by periodic mowing to destroy brush and weeds, and then by seeding more productive grasses and legumes; (3) the combination of some agricultural activities per se, such as the growing of forage crops and feed grains—corn, soybeans, sorghums, even sugar cane—with the strictly animal enterprises that long had been the predilection of those who eventually shifted to dairying; and (4) the mounting educational campaigns designed to change the food habits of adults and to get them to consume more milk.

In the years since 1950 all of these have moved along rapidly. The progress was especially marked during the 1960s. Probably one of the most important factors in the entire change was the transplantation to Brazil of a complete system of modern dairy husbandry by several thousand Dutch farmers who were resettled in São Paulo and Paraná at the Holambra[11] and other Dutch colonies in those states. But nowadays one cannot read far in the pages of Brazilian agricultural periodicals such as the national *Entensão Rural* and the *Correio Agro-Pecuario* of São Paulo, or the Sunday agricultural supplements of the country's great newspapers, without encountering evidences of current substantial endeavors to upgrade the quality of Brazil's dairy cattle. And if one visits the countryside in southern Brazil today, he will be able to see considerable evidence that the efforts are not all in vain. For example, in 1966 Dr. Harold M. Clements, Sr., of the Stephen F. Austin University in Nacogdoches, Texas, traveled extensively throughout the state of Minas Gerais to collect the materials used in his doctoral dissertation entitled "A Sociological Study of the Mechanization of Agriculture in Minas Gerais, Brazil."[12] His experiences were in sharp contrast to my own during the early 1940s (when I traveled considerably in the same territory) upon discovering that the butter and cheese I found in the markets of Rio de Janeiro were being made from daily stripping of modicums of milk from hundreds of thousands of Zebú cows that subsisted entirely upon the natural pastures. Clements frequently encountered evidences of improved dairy husbandry. Thus, even though his attention was focused primarily upon another aspect of agriculture, he made reference to milk cows on almost every page of his notes, and in not a few cases the observations pertain to fairly advanced stages of milk production. For example, the notes for his very first day in Minas Gerais, in which he traveled the highway from Rio de Janeiro to Belo Horizonte, contain some highly pertinent entries. Then, almost immediately after crossing into Minas Gerais at Afonso

Arinos, he saw evidences of decadent coffee culture and indicated that this entire section of the state once was devoted to coffee production. In 1965, however, "the hillsides were being used largely as pastures for dairy cattle (generally a mixture of Zebú and Holstein); and as we drove along, these were to be seen moving along the steep slopes, making their regular terrace-like trails. At frequent intervals all along the highway we also passed cans of milk at farm entrances and road crossings, awaiting pickup by trucks from plants processing dairy products."[13] Subsequently, as he crisscrossed the state, greatly assisted by the personnel of ACAR, the state's highly effective agricultural extension service, and frequently accompanying them on their visits to the farms, the pages of his journal became replete with observations on dairy husbandry in its various stages of development. Thus on arriving in Ouro Fino, near the border with São Paulo in the southeastern part of Minas Gerais,

> we went directly to the local office of ACAR which had been established in 1964. The local supervisor already had 130 *mutuários,* that is, farmers who received both technical and financial assistance (ACAR is interested only in properties from 10 to 100 hectares in area, whose operators have legal titles, live on the holdings, and are engaged actively in their operation).
> . . . We visited first a sítio of 50 hectares whose owner is a mutuário. . . . [He] uses an ox-drawn, wooden plow for preparing the soil; and cultivates and harvests by hand. His herd of 28 milk cows (Zebú with some admixture of Holstein) are fed shredded sugar cane, napier (grass), manioc, and corn. The appearance of most suggests the amount of the rations should be increased. Milk production averages about five liters per cow per day. Milk is poured into cans, lashed to the backs of pack mules, and taken to the highway to await the truck from the cooperative.[14]

In the same area, and even more removed from the highway, Dr. Clements visited another place containing eighty-seven hectares and devoted to the production of milk, coffee, and oranges.

> It is owned and operated by two brothers who live on the property. Although one is a graduate of an agricultural college, they frequently seek the advice of ACAR technicians. Their herd consists of 85 cows, 30 calves, and several bulls, all *suiços,*

or [Brown] Swiss dairy cattle. The milking shed, large enough
to accommodate most of the cows, is well constructed with
concrete floors and feeding troughs. By reaching over her feeding trough each cow can drink the clear water which constantly
runs through another trough parallel to it. Equipment for preparing sugar cane, napier, manioc, and corn is housed in a
building on the hillside above. Feed dropped through a chute
into carts below can be wheeled along the troughs for easy
distribution. Prepared feeding supplements are kept in a store-
room. . . . Milk is taken to the highway in a four-wheel metal
trailer hitched to a jeep. Several hillsides are covered with rows
of coffee trees, and one with orange trees. Others are in pasture.
All feed (with the exception of supplements, such as cotton seed
cake) is raised on the farm. The fact that each cow averages
eight liters of milk per day is itself indicative of better care and
more adequate feeding than on places visited previously.[15]

The same day in the same general locality, Dr. Clements went to
see

a caboclo mutuário on his ten-hectare holding. Unlike the others, this man depends entirely upon his dairy enterprise. Despite only two years of schooling, he keeps an accurate account
of feeding and milk production. Since his small holding has no
level ground, all feed crops must be grown on hillsides so steep
that the hoe is about the only feasible implement. Through hard
work and thrift (and with the financial and technical assistance
of ACAR) he has been able to accumulate within one and
one-half years a herd of 42 cows, 15 calves, and one bull. While
the animals are of the usual Zebú-Holstein mixture, the latter
predominates. . . . With attention and his care about feeding,
each of his cows gives from ten to eleven liters of milk per day.[16]

In the same general area the notes of the perceptive observer we
are quoting contain entries about "the 1,500-hectare fazenda, owned
by a wealthy Brazilian of Italian descent, who lives in the city" that
was managed by an administrator. There, "as so frequently is the
case, activities consist in a large dairy enterprise and the cultivation
of coffee and oranges," and the "even more elaborate dairy operation" on a place of eighty hectares "owned by a person of German

extraction who also lives in the city" and also "managed by an administrator." On this the cows were "all black and white, pure-bred Holstein." Then on the same date, "after dark we stopped at a large milk cooperative in São Gonçalo" where the milk was either chilled for immediate shipment to São Paulo or processed as cheese or powdered milk."[17] As he completed his efforts to take stock of the extent of the mechanization of agriculture in the southeastern part of Minas Gerais, on October 28, 1965, Dr. Clements recorded the following general observation in his journal: "It appears that the process of change from the cultivation of coffee to dairy farming (underway since the collapse of the coffee market in the early 1930's) is virtually complete. Almost all farmers have acquired dairy animals and are improving their quality. Even the small operator with his few poor cows is trying to enlarge his tiny herd and secure a bull of improved strain."[18] The entries relating to milk and milk production made in his journal by Dr. Clements as he visited other sections of the huge state of Minas Gerais are less numerous, but in all areas he encountered evidences of the development of dairy husbandry and recorded his observations relating to the same. His cogent materials are of considerable significance to all who seek to understand the important role the development of this highly productive type of farming is playing in the race between the population and the food supply in Brazil.

Dr. Clements's materials pertain only to the milk sheds of Brazil's largest cities, enormous Rio de Janeiro and São Paulo, each now a metropolitan center of well over five million inhabitants and nucleus of a metropolitan community of several million more, and the bur-geoning capital of the state of Minas Gerais, Belo Horizonte, where the city proper now contains well over a million inhabitants. It should be stressed, however, that dairy husbandry also is increasing by leaps and bounds in the vicinity of all of Brazil's rapidly increasing assortment of large urban centers. Some of the most adequate of the materials about these developments that have come to my attention are those describing the role of fairly recently established Mennonite colonies in supplying milk for Curitiba, capital of Paraná. In a care-ful and substantial study, Dr. Reynolds Herbert Minnich has sup-plied a wealth of detail about the establishment of these colonies and their system of social organization, including the dairy husbandry that is the type of farming they transplanted from Russia and forms

the economic base of their communities.[19] Dr. Minnich also participated in the very comprehensive study of one of these communities,
Witmarsum, made by the specialists in the social sciences of the
University of Paraná. This small agricultural community was formed
in 1951 about thirty-five miles west of Curitiba in the município of
Palmeira. In 1953 it contained 74 families having a total of 378
members. By 1964 the number of families had risen to 129 and the
population to 748. Dairying and enterprises complementary to it are
about the only economic activities carried on by those who make up
the colony. In 1953 these Mennonite farmers possessed a total of 450
milk cows and their cooperative sent a total of 261,489 liters of milk
to the market in Curitiba. By 1966 the number of milk cows had risen
to 1,537, and the amount of milk handled by the cooperative to
3,213,267 liters.[20]

Another excellent source of information about the progress of
dairy husbandry in modern Brazil is the *Extensão Rural,* established
in 1965 by ABCAR, Brazil's national agricultural extension service.
Few of its numbers fail to include at least one account of the increasing supply or improving quality of milk. In the September 1969 issue,
for example, is an illustrated account of ACAR, the rural extension
service of Minas Gerais, providing the credit for the purchase of
fourteen hundred pure-bred dairy cattle by the farmers of that state;
in the December issue of the same year a well-illustrated feature
story, "Cuiabá Wants More Milk of Good Quality," describes the
efforts to improve the milk supply of the capital of Mato Grosso. The
number for May 1970 contains details about the introduction of
high-grade Holstein cattle in the município of Botelhos, Minas
Gerais, and the tripling of milk production in the same, and that for
August 1970 features the construction of an immense new milk-
processing plant, the fourth largest in Brazil, under way in the município of São Gonçalo near Niterói, large satellite of the city of Rio
de Janeiro and capital of the state of Rio de Janeiro.

As indicated above in one of the quotations from Dr. Clements,
Brazil's extension service combines technical assistance and supervised credit and limits credit to farmers on places of somewhat
modest proportions. For this reason, the efforts to improve the production of milk on the great fazendas of São Paulo (where the state
agricultural extension service has not yet affiliated with the national
organization) and the other states figure very little on the pages of
Extensão Rural. This does not mean, however, that such endeavors

are lacking. Moreover, frequently such developments are grandiose.
For example, the June 29, 1970, number of *Foreign Agriculture,*
published by the foreign agricultural service of the U.S. Department
of Agriculture, contains the following item submitted by the U.S.
agricultural officer at the Consulate General in São Paulo: "On May
11, 1970, 141 head of U.S. dairy breeding cattle were ùnloaded at
Viracopas Airport, São Paulo—the largest shipment of U.S. livestock ever made to Brazil. The Holsteins, 140 heifers aged 9 to 17
months and one bull . . . were purchased by two Brazilian breeders,
one of whom is starting an entirely new dairy operation with an
all-U.S. registered Holstein herd. The cattle were selected during a
visit by one of the Brazilian buyers to some 62 farms in six U.S.
states."

These efforts to augment the supply and improve the quality of
milk in Brazil are accompanied by rapid changes in the food habits
and dietary practices of Brazil's people. Many of these changes are
the result of a huge immigration of people from Europe earlier in the
century, of the recent mushrooming of the urban populations, of
rapidly rising standards and much more slowly rising levels of living,
and of the general homogenization of Brazilian society. However,
organized educational campaigns such as "Milk Week" doubtless are
having considerable effect. In São Paulo, for example, in 1969 a Milk
Educational Campaign organized by the milk producers of that state,
with the support of the state governor, received an award as "the best
promotional campaign of the year." Some of the details about this
effort are supplied by the following translation of a couple of paragraphs from a report in the March 1970 issue of the *Correio Agro-
Precuario* of São Paulo:

> The milk education program was begun early in 1969. Its
> principal objective was to combat the prejudices and psycholog-
> ical resistances against milk, such as "milk is a drink for ba-
> bies," "milk is something extra," and "milk is fattening." The
> campaign was highly successful. The sale of milk increased. It
> was common to see men drinking milk in the city's bars. Nu-
> merous families began drinking milk with their meals, as a
> valuable additional nutrient. Organized by the P. A. Nascimen-
> to–Acar Propaganda publicity agency, the new phase of the
> campaign made use of ads in the newspapers, film strips on
> television, radio announcements, and signs on billboards, in a

major attempt to appeal to children, and through them to other consumers, emphasizing the deliciousness and the nutritious and healthful qualities of milk.

The accomplishments to date are only a beginning, but they do represent a substantial start in the production and use of a highly important food. During the 1970s the increased production of milk alone should play a great role in helping the food supply to keep pace with the growth of population and in a substantial improvement in the diet of the Brazilian people. In this connection it should be remembered that only a few parts of Brazil that are best suited for dairying are being used for that purpose, that only a beginning has been made in the improvement of pastures and the growing of forage crops, and that the upgrading of the cows that are milked still has far to go.[21] Moreover, the per capita consumption still is very low, and as late as 1966 pasteurized milk was available in only eight of the states and territories that make up the Brazilian confederation. At that time the cities of Belo Horizonte and Brasília represented the northern and westernmost outposts of this advance in milk processing, which is to say that many of Brazil's greatest cities, including Recife, Salvador, and Fortaleza, lacked such safeguards to their milk supplies. With the headway already accomplished in the densely inhabited parts of southern Brazil, and the increased efforts to expand milk production and develop milk-processing plants included in the four-year development plan, progress to overcome these deficiencies seems certain.[22]

12

Improvement in the Ways of
Farming in Latin America

Throughout large parts of Latin America, as indeed throughout much of the world, the matter of agricultural development or the lack of it reduces itself largely to the answers to the following questions. Will it be possible for any country on which attention may be focused quickly to modernize its ways of farming? Can it rapidly change from ways of getting products from the soil that are antiquated, laborious, ineffective, and often demeaning and stultifying to its workers to those that are more efficient and dignifying to those who live from work in agricultural and pastoral enterprises? Nothing is fraught with more significance for the present race between population and the food supply in Latin America than the possibilities of quick and substantial improvements in the ways of farming used in its rural districts. This is because the path to be followed has already been marked in many, many parts of the world. Especially in Canada, northwestern Europe, Australia, New Zealand, and the United States the quantities of food, feed, and fiber produced by given amounts of human energy on fixed acreages of land have, in the course of the last century, been multiplied time and time again, and the end of the advancement is not yet in sight. Even so, in a world in which hunger and starvation are the lot of hundreds of millions of people the slowness of progress in this fundamental feature of life and labor in the rural districts is dismaying. When mankind is well within the portals of the nuclear age the failure in many areas, including immense portions of Latin America, to effect substantial improvements in the ways of growing crops, producing meat and other livestock products, and transporting supplies and products between the farms and markets is appalling; it dooms millions of Latin Americans and hundreds of millions of people in other parts of the world to lives that are hardly above a mere creature level of existence.

The present writer feels fully justified in making these generalizations even though he personally has been privileged to observe many highly perfected ways of farming in widely separated parts of Latin America. Even as this chapter was being written, he visited ultramodern sugar-cane plantations in the Dominican Republic and the Cauca Valley of Colombia and saw once more some of the most effective ways of farming being used by Japanese and other farmers in the vicinity of the great city of São Paulo, Brazil. He also has seen and admired the practices currently in use on many farms in Argentina, on the splendid cotton farms in the upper part of the Magdalena Valley in Colombia, and on many other thoroughly modern farms and ranches in Mexico, Peru, Costa Rica, Venezuela, Uruguay, and Ecuador. He has observed with intense interest the effective ways of producing crops and handling livestock that are used by the Japanese colony in Brazil, the highly perfected dairying of recent Dutch immigrants in Brazil, and dozens of other effective ways of combining land, labor, capital, and management in every one of the Latin American countries. On the other hand, however, he personally has seen in many of the heavily populated portions of Latin America tens of thousands of little subsistence tracts, thousands of small and moderately sized farms, and many hundreds of haciendas, *estancias,* and *fundos* on which the ways of farming used are no more advanced than those used in ancient times. As indicated elsewhere in this volume he has been able to document the fact that in both Brazil and Colombia the overwhelming majority of all agriculturists lack agricultural implements of any kind except the ax and the hoe and that the majority of them have for use in their work no power of any kind except that supplied by their own arms and backs. And, it should be stressed, these countries by no means are the greatest laggards in the modernization of their ways of farming. Such antiquated ways of farming are prima-facie evidence that human labor is being wasted with abandon and that the input of management in various agricultural and pastoral enterprises is extremely meager. On the other hand, the room for improvement is unlimited. Just as the dissemination of modern health and sanitation measures quickly reduced the death rate throughout Latin America, instruction and training in more effective ways of getting products from the soil can greatly multiply the production of crops and livestock in the same areas.

Ways of Farming as a Sociocultural System

The concept *ways of farming* as used in this chapter requires careful definition, although its general connotations are easily understood. As is true of a system of any kind, the sociocultural system we designate as ways of farming involves an organization or ordering of its constituent parts into a functional entity, that is, into a unity that is vastly different from a mere aggregation of its components. Hence the significance of the term *system* as used here is similar to that it has in such other contexts as mechanical system, weather system, organic system, and so on. In addition, as is true of all adequate definitions, it is necessary to distinguish this specific system from all of the other entities in the group or category to which it pertains. This we attempt to do by specifying that it is made up of ideas and beliefs, cultural traits and complexes, scientific knowledge and folklore, technical skills and arts, tools and equipment, implements and machines, draft animals and other domestic livestock, habits and prejudices, techniques and practices, and so on, used by the inhabitants of a given locality in order to get crop and livestock products from the soil. In a word, it is a sociocultural system and not some other kind of a system precisely because the essential components involved are human beings, social groupings, social classes, cultural traits, cultural complexes, and other strictly societal and cultural elements. Furthermore, it should be emphasized that any one of the ways of farming is a highly crystallized or institutionalized part of the social order. In all parts of the world there is considerable standardization at the neighborhood level in the customary ways of preparing the seedbeds, controlling weeds, harvesting the crops, transporting the products, caring for livestock and poultry, and moving things to and from the local markets. Finally, in any given rural community the prevailing values usually are highly favorable to the continuance of the traditional ways of growing crops, handling the livestock, and consuming or marketing the products.

It should be apparent that the sociocultural system denoted as ways of farming must be thought of in a way that will include a very broad range of social and cultural phenomena. Among one of the remaining small Brazilian or Ecuadorian Indian villages, for example, the principal components of the system in use may be the digging stick used by the women of the community, usually a few domesticated fowl, several domesticated plants such as maize or beans, and a set of magical or religious beliefs and practices the people firmly believe will help insure germination of the seeds, promote fertility, and ward off things that might imperil the crops. In sharp contrast the system in use in other parts of the same countries may involve thoroughly modern scientific principles of plant breeding and propagation, the most up-to-date practices of animal husbandry, the utilization of the tractor and its associated implements in tillage and harvest, reliance upon the motor truck for transportation, and the employment of the airplane and helicopter in the performance of such farm tasks as dusting and spraying and even seeding. Between the two poles mentioned here, namely the agricultural lore and traditional practices of the people in the primitive community at the one extreme and the rational application of scientific knowledge, the principles of engineering, and the highly developed managerial skills of the successful operator of a substantial family-sized farm at the other, lies the entire range of mankind's social and cultural development.

For those who would grasp the opportunity offered by the improvement of the ways of farming as a means of enabling the food supply to outpace the growth of population in Latin America in the immediate future, it is imperative that the more advanced and perfected of the various ways of farming be considered as the moving forces, or the independent variable, in contemporary programs of agricultural development. In every country both the national agencies and the representatives of the international organizations working there must give this factor the importance it deserves in the presently widespread efforts to replace or correct the age-old deficiencies in the ways the farmers go about extracting products from the soil. As is indicated elsewhere in this volume, however, this can be accomplished only if the entire rural sociocultural system that is based upon large landed estates, and the resulting condition in which the vast majority of all those who live from agriculture are kept in the menial condition of mere agricultural laborers, can be replaced

by a system in which family-sized farms come to be the central core
of the arrangement and the large majority of the heads of all farm
families are actual farm operators rather than laborers. If these
efforts can be moderately successful, so that the typical farmer in
each Latin American country comes to use ways of farming somewhat comparable in effectiveness with those of the more advanced
farmers in his own country, the increases in the production of food,
feed, and fiber will be startling.

The Six Major Ways of Farming

Even before some of the major recent advancements in the ways
of farming employed in the United States had been made, there were
many expressions of the tremendous progress made in the ways of
getting products from the soil during the last century or so of history.
For example, the authors of one of the pertinent articles in what for
many years had been a standard reference book for use in high
schools asserted that in 1940 a farmer in the United States could care
for 750 acres of land as easily as George Washington's father could
cultivate 50 acres. Moreover, those responsible for this statement
further indicated that the primitive man would have required an
equivalent amount of labor merely to get a crop from a single acre.
For present purposes we need not seek to determine the accuracy of
these estimates nor to indicate how much persons not actually engaged in farming contribute to the production of crops and livestock
on the modern farm. Even if a tremendous margin of error is allowed, the fact remains that during the nineteenth and twentieth
centuries those living from agricultural activities in the United States
and a few other countries have made tremendous advancement in
their ways of farming. And it should be stressed time and time again
that for the most part the tried and tested improvements in the ways
of farming only recently have begun to make a substantial impact
upon life and labor in most of the Latin American countries. But the
process of change is now under way in many places and within the
next few decades improved ways of farming are almost certain to
change drastically the amounts of crops and livestock products taken
from the land. In order to help take stock of these changes, however,
it is essential to have a classification of the basic ways in which
mankind has gone about agricultural and pastoral activities.

As indicated above, anyone who travels throughout Latin America and other parts of the world will encounter the most diverse methods by which men and women cooperate with nature in the production of food, feed, and fiber. These range all the way from extremely simple activities, for which very fine distinctions must be made in order to separate them from the mere collecting acts that take place in a preagricultural society, to the highly mechanized and motorized procedures now in use in a few parts of Mexico, Costa Rica, Peru, Argentina, and the other Latin American countries. If they are properly classified and arranged, the resulting types also are suggestive of the lines of social and cultural evolution through which men and women have increased their control over nature, even during those prehistoric times for which there are no written records. From this point of view each of the six major ways of farming discussed in several places in this volume may be thought of as a stage in the development of civilization, since the line of development undoubtedly was from the simple to the more complex. One must be quick to add, however, that this does not imply that any given society must pass sequentially through each of the six stages as described and discussed in the pages that follow. We have come to recognize, for example, that it seems practically impossible to introduce the system we designate as advanced plow culture in any of the countries that lack such a cultural heritage, except through the process of actually transferring farmers, immigrants habituated to its components and procedures, from one country to another. On the other hand, in the present stage of mechanical development in the nonagricultural portions of any given Latin American country, it presently is relatively easy to transplant a complete system of mechanized and motorized farming.

The six principal ways of farming used in the classification I have developed and applied rather widely are as follows: (1) riverbank plantings; (2) felling and burning or "fire agriculture"; (3) hoe culture; (4) rudimentary plow culture; (5) advanced plow culture; and (6) mechanized or motorized farming. In the following section an attempt is made to present the essential information about the nature of each of these, its present role in Latin America, and the extent to which earlier and less effective ways of farming are being replaced by those that enhance the productivity of men and women and the land they use.

The Replacement of Antiquated with More Effective Ways of Farming

In the 1960s substantial progress was made in many parts of Latin America in the replacement of antiquated and ineffective ways of farming with those that yield far greater amounts of product per worker and per acre. There is reason to hope that this process can be greatly accelerated in the immediate future, thereby playing a very important role in the race between population and the food supply in one of the world's great regions. In the following paragraphs an attempt is made to indicate rather completely the essential features of each of the six basic ways of farming and to comment upon the extent to which each of them is gaining or losing ground in the Latin American countries.

First of all, however, it seems necessary to indicate that before anyone can understand the more primitive ways of farming he or she must be able to make a clear distinction between agriculture as such and the still more elementary stage of economic activity, that of hunting, fishing, and collecting, that preceded it. Offhand one has a right to expect such precise information in any general treatment of the history of agriculture. Nevertheless, such essential information is not readily found. Rather, in the writings of those considered to be authorities in the field the distinction is likely to be glossed over in a way comparable to what is done in *Compton's Pictorial Encyclopedia and Fact-Index*. According to this widely used source, "A stick was the first hand tool used to scratch the surface of the ground before planting, and a forked stick, held in the ground by the plowman while the oxen dragged it ahead, was the first plow."[1]

This statement, however, and thousands of others similar to it, are based on a rather naïve assumption that agriculture began with cultivation. It conveniently ignores the cultural accumulations during thousands of years of experience by men and women before the latter used any kind of tools or implements in the preparation of a seedbed or in the care of the plants grown on it. To indicate the gross superficiality of such statements one need merely to ask how, when, and where mankind acquired all of the ideas, knowledge, and skills that their authors take for granted. Do such things as the saving of seeds, the act of burying them in locations where they can take root and grow, and the engineering skills involved in the simplest acts of tillage fall in the category of spontaneous behavior? And in the same connection, what about the knowledge of how to shape and use the crudest of plows, the domestication and training of the oxen, and the development of even the crudest of hitching equipment? Each and every one of these had to grow out of a long series of more elementary human activities and even simpler cultural traits and complexes during the very lengthy period in which women were acquiring the knowledge of farming that eventually came to outweigh either the activities of their menfolk in hunting and fishing or that of members of both sexes in collecting nature's free gifts of seeds, nuts, fruits, and tubers.

Woman's first farming was only slightly removed from those collecting activities, and certainly the great Amazon Basin of South America was one of the places in which this significant step was taken, along with other independent developments of the same kind in such other parts of the world as Egypt, Asia Minor, and China. There seems every reason to suppose that woman first interfered or cooperated with the processes of nature by thinning out some of the competing plants in small clumps of the same from which she had learned to expect a harvest of seeds or tubers. This activity alone, though, did not convert her into an agriculturist. Before she could become a farmer she had to get and apply the idea of taking some of the seeds and tubers collected from the wild plants and depositing them in places where they could germinate, sprout, take root, and grow. Then and only then did she enter upon her long career as a farmer, and then and only then did she start mankind on the long rough road that would develop a civilization.

Riverbank planting. As indicated above, the great Amazon Basin certainly was one of the places in which the transition of the purely collecting economy to one of agriculture took place. In this great heartland of the South American continent, the rivers rise for half of the year and then fall during the other six months. Annually, following the flood stage, the ebb of the stream leaves along its banks soft, pliable, loamy banks of soil completely prepared as seedbeds. Long before there was tillage or cultivation of any kind, woman discovered that merely by saving seeds and using the ball of her foot to sink them into the soft surfaces along the bank, she could greatly multiply the gifts of nature. Such activities surely must be counted as agricultural, although the way of farming involved is the simplest

. one possible. This kind of agriculture involves no implements whatsoever, not even the crude digging stick.

After I personally had become acquainted with this way of farming during a visit to the Amazon Valley in 1942, I sought diligently
in the writings of the great naturalists who had spent much of their
lives in the area for scientific descriptions of the process we are
considering. Unfortunately these efforts were largely in vain. In the
writings of Alfred Russell Wallace, however, there is evidence that
at the same time he independently was formulating the theory of
evolution generally associated solely with the name of Charles Darwin, he had observed the essentials of the sociocultural subsystem
designated here as riverbank planting. Thus he relates that in the
course of some of the "dull and dreary evenings" he spent at Javita,
a small settlement near the channel that links the Orinoco River
system with that of the Amazon, he amused himself and passed the
time by composing blank verse descriptive of the life of the Indians
in the settlement. The following lines from one of his poetic efforts
deal with the way of farming we are attempting to describe:

> The women dig the mandiocca root,
> And with much labour make of it their bread.
> These plant the young shoots in the fertile earth—
> Earth all untill'd, to which the plough, or spade,
> Or rake, or harrow, are alike unknown.[2]

Moreover, the possibilities of introducing vastly more effective ways
of farming than this riverbank type, and the felling and burning that
also was widespread in the area, undoubtedly was weighing heavily
in his thoughts when he wrote the following lines:

> When I consider the excessively small amount of labour
> required in this country, to convert the virgin forest into green
> meadows and fertile plantations, I almost long to come over
> with half-a-dozen friends, disposed to work, and enjoy the
> country; and show the inhabitants how soon an earthly paradise
> might be created, which they had never even conceived capable
> of existing.
> ... here the "primeval" forest can be converted into rich
> pasture and meadow land, into cultivated fields, gardens, and
> orchards, containing every variety of produce, with half the

labour, and, what is of more importance, in less than half the time that would be required at home, even though there we had clear, instead of forest ground to commence upon. It is true that ground once rudely cleared, in the manner of the country, by merely cutting down the wood and burning it as it lies, will, if left to itself, in a single year, be covered with a dense shrubby vegetation; but if the ground is cultivated and roughly weeded, the trunks and stumps will have so rotted in two or three years, as to render their complete removal an easy matter, and then a fine crop of grass succeeds; and, with cattle upon it, no more care is required, as no shrubby vegetation again appears. . . . Now, I unhesitatingly affirm, that two or three families, containing half-a-dozen working and industrious men and boys, and being able to bring a capital in goods of fifty pounds, might, in three years, find themselves in the possession of all I have mentioned. [Orchards, groves of coffee and cacao trees, oranges and other fruit trees; abundance of pineapples, melons, and watermelons; abundant fields of rice and corn; plenty of onions, beans, and many other vegetables. All of these would thrive luxuriantly, if cultivated, but "the ground is never turned up, and manure never applied; if both were done, it is probable that the labour would be richly repaid." In addition, he mentioned that his settlers could have plenty of cattle, sheep, goats, and pigs, for "nobody ever gives them anything to eat, and they always do well. Poultry of all kinds thrive."][3]

There are several distinctive variants of the riverbank way of farming, although as far as I have been able to determine the most important of these has not been used in any of the Latin American countries. This is the practice, all-important in the Nile Valley in ancient times, of broadcasting seeds over the flood plain as the water recedes and then driving oxen around over the muddy surfaces for the purpose of sinking the seeds of wheat, barley, and so on, into the ground.[4] Another of the variants, however, is of considerable importance in drought-plagued northeastern Brazil and may be employed elsewhere in the more arid sections of Latin America. This consists of dibbling seeds into the beds of the washes and the courses of streams that flow intermittently. Often this enables some foodstuffs to be produced, but if a rain comes and the water flows again before the crops are mature, all is lost.

Riverbank plantings make up the simplest and most elementary of all the ways in which men and women have a part in fostering the processes of nature to augment the food supply. Therefore, in the process of development it is the one that gives way before all the others. In the decades ahead it will become more and more difficult to find cases in which this way of farming is the sole or major reliance of any of the communities throughout Latin America.

Felling and burning ("fire agriculture"). In some places hoe culture may have developed directly out of the riverbank way of farming, but it is unlikely that this was the case in aboriginal America. The use of the system designated as felling and burning or "fire agriculture" was so widespread at the time of the conquest and continues in use today in so many parts of South and Central America that it would be presumptious to think of hoe culture as being very widely used in the Americas before 1500. The ways of farming used by the Incas in Peru and in the central parts of the Aztec Empire in Mexico probably are the major exceptions to the rule, although the Chibchas in the highlands of Colombia also definitely had advanced considerably in the use of digging sticks and other hand implements in the actual cultivation of the soil, that is, in the way of farming we term hoe culture. The Mayas in Central America and Yucatan, on the other hand, probably depended almost entirely upon felling and burning as the method of preparing the ground for the seeds.

It is easily demonstrated that soft, pliable surfaces of earth (dirt so friable that it easily is stirred merely with a sweep of the big toe) are left where a fire has found plentiful fuel. Many such places are found where nature alone, merely through the persistence of a dry season, the aging of trees, the actions of strong winds, and the work of lightning, bears undisputed sway. Hence, it was a very short step in the development of civilization between the stage in which the rivers alone were relied upon for the preparation of seedbeds to one in which fire consciously was used for a similar purpose. In any case, tremendous areas in South and Central America, the Antilles, and also Africa, Asia, and Oceania are still occupied by peoples who either depend largely upon a system of felling and burning in agricultural production or who have only recently changed to more effective ways of farming. Even in 1975, on a trip on which many parts of South America were revisited, I saw many evidences of the persistence of this precultivation stage of agricultural existence (in the

Amazon Basin, in the southwestern part of the advanced state of Pananá, Brazil, and in Paraguay). However, in many others, such as the parts of central Goiás surrounding Brasília where when I first saw them in the 1940s "fire agriculture" reigned almost supreme, hoe culture and mechanized farming are in general use.

The details concerning the way in which felling and burning is used in the production of food crops need not concern us here. It seems essential, however, to dwell for a few moments upon the most accurate and meaningful designation to be used for this way of farming since a variety of terms are used to denote the system, some of which we insist are completely inaccurate and misleading. There can be little quarrel with the names given the processes involved in Spanish (*rozar*) and Portuguese (*derrubadas e queimadas*) since both signify felling and burning. I myself am responsible for introducing the term "fire agriculture," and I did so in the first edition of my volume *Brazil: People and Institutions* (1946) as the title of a chapter in which I tried to give the details about a widespread way of farming that had little in common with the ways of getting products from the soil that had been transplanted from Europe. In so doing, I sought to challenge anyone who glanced at the table of contents of the book at least to read enough of the chapter to learn what it was all about. In that treatise, however, and everything else I have written on the subject I have carefully avoided the use of certain other designations for felling and burning, especially the labels "shifting cultivation," "slash and burn," and the "milpa system." The first of these, one of the most widely used, is completely inappropriate and misleading, since no tillage whatsoever is employed in the system it is used to denote. Its use reminds one of the anecdote about the small boy in the southern part of the United States who was having breakfast at the home of a neighbor. In an endeavor to see that her little guest had all of the essentials to go along with the hot biscuits he had been served, his hostess inquired, "Would you like some molasses?" To this the little boy replied with a question of his own: "How can I have mo' 'lasses when I ain't had any 'lasses yet?" It is difficult to conceive of *shifting* cultivation when no cultivation whatsoever is involved.

Slash and burn, likewise, is almost sure to give an entirely inaccurate image of the processes actually involved. In Brazil, for example, I personally have seen as many as four axmen simultaneously cutting at the base of a gigantic tree, the felling of which took all four many hours of work to accomplish. And in one of my endeavors to educate readers who had become accustomed to referring to the process of felling and burning as "slash and burn" agriculture, I translated the following description of the process as I had observed it in many parts of Colombia: "The work commences: the file of peons begin the felling of the forest; the small trees submissively give way to the stroke of the machete, the small shoots bow miserably like the masses before a dictator; but the towering giants, the *diomates* and the *guayacanes,* fearlessly resist the ax, but they always fall, with a thundering crash that terrorizes all the wild animals and reverberates throughout the forest."[5] Of course, if there were a race of Paul Bunyons or Herculeses in the rural districts of Latin America, one could imagine them going about the work of slashing down and burning the forests of South and Central America, but in all of my own travels I always failed to encounter this.

Finally, in Mexico and Central America what is known as the milpa system refers to farming procedures in which the machete is used annually to clear the weeds, dried cornstalks, and so on, from a small section of the mountainside, preparatory to another planting. It has little in common with the way of farming we are considering here.

For centuries felling and burning has been one of the principal methods of securing products from the soil throughout the majority of the territory of the twenty Latin American countries. At present, however, its distribution is being substantially lessened, and the shift from this extremely wasteful (of timber resources and human energy) way of farming to more effective and productive procedures is a major factor in the increased production of food in Latin America.

Hoe culture. Once woman had learned, through trial and error, that open, spongy bits of land are favorable to the growth of plants, she was on the verge of taking another fundamental step in the long, oft-interrupted march of the development of civilization. At various times and places quite independently of one another, many peoples have had the idea of using the sharp points of sticks to stir the soil preparatory to planting it with seeds or tubers. In many cases the genesis of such tillage probably was stimulated by the use of sticks, bones, and shells to spare the fingers and fingernails in digging for roots and tubers. In any event no great intellectual or cultural development is required for a man or woman to pick up, retain for repeated usages, and even attempt to improve somewhat a piece of bone, a shell, or a pointed stick. Many of the anthropoids demonstrate an ability to select and use tools of this and greater degrees of complexity, even though none of them seems to have begun the process of cultural development by teaching another of his kind to do the same thing. When the primitive farmers got the idea of adding a sharp, flat piece of bone, a shell, a sharp stone, or a piece of metal to the end of a digging stick, the hoe was invented. With this implement, plus a knowledge of fertilization (such as placing a fish in each hill of corn planted), genuine cultivation and permanent agriculture were achieved.

Beyond all doubt highly improved digging sticks and crude hoes of one kind or another were widely used throughout the Americas before the arrival of the Spaniards and the Portuguese. But the virtual lack of any metals that would serve as blades for hoes precluded the perfection of any highly developed implements of this type. The digging sticks used in the densely populated highlands of the Andes by the Incas, however, are one example of cultural evolution to a point near the possible maximum. With this instrument, merely a sharpened stick to which another piece of wood was attached about a foot above the end so that the foot could help apply the energy needed to force the point into the ground, the Indians made rich productive fields out of the thousands of square miles of terraces they constructed in what are now Peru and its neighboring countries. It is common to refer to this improved digging stick as a "foot plow," although it would be better designated as an extremely crude spade. One should hasten to add, however, that this implement was not widely disseminated throughout the Americas at the time of the conquest and that the use of it did not become a part of the cultural heritages of the Andean peoples who lived in what are now Colombia and Venezuela. In the 1940s, for example, I personally observed in Nariño and other parts of Colombia as many as fifty workers, all equipped merely with digging sticks, working in unison on the hillsides under the direction of a majordomo.

The heavy, broad-bladed hoe of steel, almost a "grubbing hoe," introduced by the Spaniards and Portuguese quickly became all-important in many parts of what are today the Latin American countries. The Indians and mestizos who worked on the estates of the Europeans and their descendants were instructed in its use, and it also was quickly taken up by those farming for themselves in the areas dominated by the white men. There its major competitor, in addition to the traditional felling and burning in the forested areas, was the way of farming we designate as rudimentary plow culture, wherein the crude old wooden plow and oxen were the core components. For about four centuries these two systems were responsible for the ineffective use or waste of the energies of many millions of humble rural workers. In the second half of the twentieth century, both public and private programs for the improvement of agriculture are necessarily largely concerned with the substitution of more advanced ways of farming for the hoe culture that has dominated the picture for several hundred years. At present the transition from hoe culture to mechanized farming is substantial, with the two intermediate stages discussed below being skipped entirely.

Rudimentary plow culture. Long before mankind in any part of the world had developed an alphabet to make possible reading and writing and the keeping of historical records, peoples in several parts of the world had transformed the forked sticks they were using as primitive grubbing hoes into the rudest possible types of plows. Such a forked stick, so shaped that one person could apply energy by pulling and another by pushing, was of course the basic instrument in this momentous discovery. There may have been cases, however, in which a plow was developed out of a hoe. In any case, throughout the Americas the lack of draft animals (except the dog, which could draw only a small sled or a travois, and the llama, which was trained to carry a light pack) precluded the development of any plow in what is now Latin America. This great agency of civilization was unknown there until the coming of the Spaniards and Portuguese. Then the type introduced had to be the old wooden variety that merely scratches the surface of the earth, rooting as it goes, because in 1500 neither the people of Spain nor those of Portugal knew of any plow more advanced than the kind used in Biblical times.

The plows introduced into the Spanish and Portuguese colonies, like those of ancient Mesopotamia and ancient Egypt and those still in use in some parts of Brazil and many parts of Spanish America, were primitive and extremely inefficient. They merely root along, laboriously tearing and digging the soil, and hardly deserve to share a common name with the modern, mathematically designed, metal instruments that glide, cut, and neatly turn the earth. Nevertheless, the fact that draft animals, even the lumbering ox or the water buffalo in Asia, are used to supplement the energy supplied by men and women themselves represents a tremendous development over hoe culture and the still more primitive system of felling and burning. In no sense, however, should these words be interpreted as a defense of the continued use of the old wooden plow and of the ox as the source of the power to propel it. I personally have had abundant opportunity from 1935 on in all of the countries from Mexico to Chile to observe that oxen can never be used very effectively when hitched to a wooden plow in the preparation of the land for the seed. And my spine has been chilled time and time again when, with complete disregard of the ABC's of engineering, these lumbering beasts are hitched to complex and finely balanced mechanical systems such as the mowing machine and the grain harvester.

The Spaniards, and also the Portuguese, introduced the horse into the Americas, and that noble steed has played a very important part in the history of the New World from 1500 on. However, the breeds of this animal brought to Mexico and Central and South America during the colonial period included none that was adapted for use as a draft animal; they were kept and used strictly for riding purposes. Horses were not even used as pack animals, for although the Spaniards and Portuguese depended mostly upon packtrains rather than vehicles of any type (except the crude oxcart to a limited extent) for transportation purposes, mules were used exclusively. Just as the even-gaited horse was never hitched to the rudimentary plow in Egypt, Mesopotamia, and even the Roman world, the same was true in Spain and Portugal and the colonies of both down to the present time, with very few exceptions. In all of the great civilizations of antiquity the horse enjoyed the high social status of his lord and master, whose war chariot he drew, whom he carried as a charger, and whose grave he came to share. The mere thought of such a noble animal becoming demeaned by drawing a plow or a cart or performing any other work connected with agriculture would have been abhorrent to those in all parts of the world, including the Iberian Peninsula, in which the Roman value system prevailed.

Until the last few decades rudimentary plow culture, with its primitive plow, rude oxcarts for transportation, and reliance upon the sickle for use in taking the harvest, has been used widely throughout Latin America. Only in areas in which large colonies of European immigrants have transplanted the ways of farming to which they had been accustomed in their homelands (as has been the case in Argentina, southern Brazil, Uruguay, and southern Chile, especially) has rudimentary plow culture been replaced by advanced plow culture. Elsewhere its replacement, now going on rather rapidly, has been through the substitution of mechanized farming.

Advanced plow culture. The fifth of the ways of farming, designated as advanced plow culture, has been the most important development in the history of agriculture and therefore of primordial significance in the development of civilization. This is the system that made it possible for a relatively small proportion of the population to produce the food, feed, and fiber used by all. In so doing, it permitted the bulk of man's energy and effort to be released from the performance of manual tasks required for mere survival and directed to managerial and other varieties of mental work. Advanced plow culture accomplished an enormous increase in the annual production per man, thus enabling large portions of the population to become occupied in nonagricultural pursuits. Within the farming industry itself, it set the stage for mechanized or motorized farming.

The core components of advanced plow culture are more numerous, more highly specialized, and much more highly integrated than those of rudimentary plow culture or any of the three still more antiquated ways of farming. They include the metal turning plow, the draft horse as the source of power, the horse collar and many other pieces of equipment used in harnessing and hitching horses to machines and vehicles, and, of the utmost importance, the use of the wheel in sets of four as expressed by the farm wagon. It is interesting to note that the Romans knew of the separate parts (except the horse collar) of the system under consideration and perhaps even more interesting, from the standpoint of the dynamics of sociocultural change, that they did not undertake to bring them together into a functioning entity. The same is true of the peoples who succeeded them in the control of the Mediterranean world, including the Spaniards and the Portuguese. Because of this, rudimentary plow culture represented the most highly perfected way of farming that the conquerors from the Iberian Peninsula could transplant in the Americas. In brief, those who supplied the Spanish and Portuguese parts of the New World cultures during the colonial period themselves never began the transition from hoe culture and rudimentary plow culture until well along in the twentieth century. This fact alone explains why until very recently practically all of the Latin American countries fell into the category of "developing nations" when that neologism came to be applied, from about 1950 on, to most of the countries in the world.

Northwestern Europe is the area in which advanced plow culture was developed into a functioning system through the invention and perfection of the horse collar, the break with the tradition of assigning upper-class status to the horse and its subsequent use as a draft animal, the perfection of the turning plow, and the development of the four-wheeled farm wagon. In the United States, especially the northern colonies (and subsequently states), and Canada, both of which received huge transplantations of European culture, the process of improving the system moved ahead rapidly. Hundreds of fundamental improvements were made in the plow and other implements, in wheeled vehicles, in harnessing and hitching equipment, and especially in the more efficient use and management of labor (through the family-sized farms). Among the most notable of the improvements were the perfection by John Deere of the steel plow, which would scour in the rich, heavy soils of midwestern prairies, the solution of the problems of a sulky plow about 1885, the invention of the mowing machine to replace the scythe in the cutting of forage crops and of the mechanical harvester for cutting fields of grain, and the development of improved and more specialized breeds of livestock (horses, cattle, swine, poultry, and sheep). In fact, all along the agricultural front in the United States and Canada great strides were made in the perfection of advanced plow culture, aided also by exchanges with the countries of northwestern Europe, Australia, and New Zealand.

Unfortunately, except by the immigration of European farmers to some locations in Latin America as mentioned above, it proved almost impossible to disseminate the improvements involved in all of this in the Latin American countries. This was not because no attempts were made. In Colombia alone dozens of attempts were made to introduce the improved plow, and I even had a hand in some of them myself.[6] Unfortunately, at the time none of us involved in the endeavors appreciated the fact that just the introduction of the plow alone into areas in which rudimentary plow culture as a system prevailed resulted in little or no improvement. The mere substitution of the metal plow for the wooden implement produces a cumbersome and laborious combination involving oxen that pull with jerky movements, the barest excuses for hitching equipment, and, most important of all, a plowman who has never passed through as a youth the six or eight years of apprenticeship required to master the art of plowing. Under such circumstances the steel plow is used as if it were a rooting instrument. Before many days have passed its beam is sprung beyond all remedy, its point and share are blunted or broken, and its moldboard is badly corroded. In all of the endeavors, carried on at various times and places in Colombia alone for over a century, none of those involved recognized that the plow is just one of the parts of a large, finely adjusted, and highly integrated sociocultural system.

Hence, advanced plow culture never was and offers little chance of becoming a significant stage in the improvement of the ways of farming in most parts of Latin America. However, because the perfection of the equipment used in this way of getting products from the soil was the indispensable base on which mechanized farming was built, eventually it became highly significant for all of the Latin American countries as well as for all the other "underdeveloped" parts of the world.

Mechanized or motorized farming. Mechanized or motorized ways of farming began making real headway in the midwestern and western parts of the United States and the adjacent provinces in Canada at about the time of the First World War, and after 1930 the use of the tractor and its associated implements rapidly became general throughout the two countries. At the same time somewhat similar developments got under way in Great Britain and some other portions of western Europe. These successes came, however, only with the perfection of the internal combustion engine and its application in the automobile, motor truck, and tractor, and only after about a century of efforts (especially in England, some of the northwestern states in the United States, and the prairie provinces of Canada) to use the steam engine to supply the energy needed in agricultural activities. As is well known, the steam-powered threshing machine did play a tremendous part in the handling of wheat, oats, barley, and other grains, but efforts to use this source of power either in mobile units or with elaborate contrivances of cables and pulleys attached to stationary engines largely came to naught. The quest was on in earnest to find a mechanical substitute for the horse, however, and when engines that would drive automobiles were perfected the use of engines of this type in farm tractors was not far behind. A few of the more important landmarks in this important development have been described in a publication of the Farm and Industrial Equipment Institute.[7]

1. As a mobile source of power for the farms, steam had serious deficiencies, and something better was needed.

2. In 1892 J. I. Case Company built the first gasoline-powered engine for a tractor, but it required ten years more before it could be applied practically in farming.

3. The name "tractor" was originally applied by the White-Parr Company in 1906 to its first successful machine, "Old No. 1." It had four iron wheels, weighed twenty thousand pounds, and developed between 22 and 45 horsepower.

4. Henry Ford, who had experimented with steam traction engines before he turned his attention to the automobile, developed a lighter tractor in 1908.

5. In 1909 thirty companies manufactured tractors and sold about two thousand of them.

6. By 1917 designs were completed for the Fordson, the first mass-produced tractor, and the next year the built-in "power take-off" was developed. This meant that by means of a specially designed shaft the tractor's engine could be used to furnish directly the power for a wide variety of implements (binders, combines, mowers, windrowers, corn pickers, cotton strippers, etc.).

7. Rubber-tired tractors were introduced by Allis-Chalmers in 1932, an improvement that contributed tremendously to speed up plowing, cultivating, and other farm operations.

Certainly by the 1930s in most of the United States and large sections of Canada a stage in the ways of farming had been reached that deserves the designation of mechanized farming. In this system, in which light, finely adjusted, and powerful machines and implements of various sizes are the core components, the ordinary farm family uses the most modern accomplishments of science and engineering as it goes about the work of tilling the soil. The tractor furnishes the power for most of the operations, but its contributions are supplemented by those of motor trucks and automobiles for transportation and a host of electrically driven machines for milking, pumping water, distributing feed, and so forth. Ever greater specialization in machines and tasks is the order of the day.

In a large measure the implements and machines used in mechanized farming are, as suggested above, improved larger and lighter versions of those that were developed to a high degree of perfection in the advanced plow culture system. They are geared to higher speeds, subject to more precise adjustments, made of more durable metals, and adapted to many more farm operations than those in the earlier stages of development. However, each year the machines and implements become more and more specialized.

During the 1970s the mechanization of agriculture is forging ahead throughout Latin America. Even the tremendous increase in the price of petroleum in 1973 and 1974 has been unable to halt its progress, although in many of the countries, unlike the situation in Venezuela and Ecuador, most of the oil and oil products must be imported. It is evident that the system as a whole is transplanted intact, and this is relatively easy, providing the finances are available to pay for all of the components. No one attempts to take merely one part of the system and substitute it for a part of one of the less developed systems, as was the case with the metal turning plow. Because the affluent families own and control most of the most fertile and the best located land, and because they also have the capital and credit needed, the transplantation of mechanized farming is relatively simple and uncomplicated. Any time a member of one of the well-to-do families gets the idea to plunge into the production of cotton, rice, sugar cane, or some other staple the coast is clear. Almost overnight a broad expanse of what for four hundred years may have been merely unimproved pasture for scrub livestock may become a luxuriant field of rice, cotton, or sugar cane.

In most places as yet only the more general-purpose equipment seems to have figured in the transplantations. The highly perfected implements and machines used in hay making are rarely seen, and the same is true of those designed and perfected to harvest and load potatoes, beets, and other root crops. In fact, highly sophisticated machines to pick corn or even the far-less-complicated mechanical cane cutters are not widely disseminated, in all likelihood partly because large gangs of unskilled farm laborers are relied upon to cut the cane and because the production of corn is not a large-scale enterprise in most of the countries. Even so, the use of the tractor and other mechanical farm equipment is contributing immensely to the increased production of food, feed, and fiber throughout Latin America, and in this way mechanized farming is playing a very important role in the race between population and the food supply. In some countries it actually is permitting a substantial increase in the per capita consumption; in others it is helping to postpone the reduced levels of consumption that otherwise probably would have to take place. Finally, the fact that the introduction and use of the more highly specialized types of machines and implements are still to come portends that for the next few decades improvements in the ways of farming will be a major feature in the agricultural development of the Latin American countries. In the years ahead all of the equipment designed and perfected to enable the farm operator himself to do all of the things in a complicated set of farm operations, aided at most by one other person, will make its way into the systems of production used on many farms. Large gangs of unskilled farm laborers rigidly regimented in their work should become less and less prominent features of the patterns of life and labor throughout the twenty countries, for indeed the mechanized way of farming promises to be among the more revolutionary sets of forces ever introduced into the area to the south and east of the Rio Grande.

The Outlook

From what has been said in this chapter, it is hoped that we have shown that the changes now taking place in the ways of farming are among the more positive features of the great race between population and the food supply throughout the Latin American countries. This, however, gives no basis for complacency about the future. With the rate of population increase presently running at almost 3 percent per year, even with prodigious strides in the modernization of the ways of farming (along with improved combinations of enterprises on the farms and ranches, more widespread ownership and control of the rights to the land, the reduction of the importance of farm laborers and an increase in the proportions of farm operators in the rural population, and all the other central features of a program of agrarian reform), the time is running out in which the birth rate must be brought under control. The alternative is that many of the countries will find themselves saddled with the problem of overpopulation to go along with that of underdevelopment. Moreover, until the birth rate is reduced, the ratio of consumers (those under fifteen) to producers (roughly those between fifteen and sixty-five) will continue to be exceedingly high. We end this chapter and this book, however, with the thought that improvement in the ways of farming can do much to give the breathing time in which some changes in the birth rate may be achieved to offset those that have already been accomplished in the reduction of the death rate. By eliminating the extremely wasteful system of felling and burning and abandoning once and for all the wooden plow, the lumbering ox, the crude oxcart, and all that goes with them in two very antiquated ways of farming, some of the principal obstacles to increased production of food, feed, and fiber can be overcome. To do this, mechanization of agriculture must be greatly advanced, not merely in its general aspects in which the tractor and some of the principal attachments are accompanied by vast amounts of hand labor in cutting cane, picking cotton, controlling weeds, and so on, but through the introduction and use of many of the more intricate and specialized machines and operations as well. The man with the hoe and most of the features of hoe culture should be eliminated as rapidly as possible. By this rapid advancement in the substitution of the most advanced ways of farming for the antiquated traditional ones, the food supply in Latin America in the immediate future may be increased even more rapidly than the population is growing. Only time can tell how well this opportunity to adjust will be used by the peoples who live below the Rio Grande.

Notes

Chapter 2

1. Cf. T. Lynn Smith, *Brazil: People and Institutions* (Baton Rouge: Louisiana State University Press, 1946), pp. 160–64, and the corresponding sections in the second, third, and fourth (1972) editions of the same.

2. For some of the detailed data on this aspect of Brazil's population policy, see ibid., 4th edition, chapter 8; and for a classic account of the British blockade, see Edward Wilberforce, *Brazil Viewed through a Naval Glass with Notes on Slavery and the Slave Trade* (London: Longman, Green, Brown, and Longmans, 1856).

3. Cf. T. Lynn Smith and Paul E. Zopf, Jr., *Demography: Principles and Methods* (Philadelphia: F. A. Davis Company, 1970), pp. 534–44.

4. The data given here were secured from the 1969 issue of the *Anuário Estatístico do Brasil* (Rio de Janeiro: Instituto Brasileiro de Geografia e Estatística, 1960), pp. 144, 162.

5. For some information on these movements see T. Lynn Smith, "The Role of Internal Migration in Population Redistribution in Brazil," *Revista International de Sociologia* 29 (January–April 1971): 109–14.

6. For descriptions of life in the small towns and villages in this part of Brazil as it was in the nineteenth century, see George Gardner, *Travels in the Interior of Brazil,* vol. 2 (London: Reeve, Benham, and Reeve, 1849), chapters 9 and 10; and James W. Wells, *Three Thousand Miles through Brazil,* vol. 2 (London: Sampson, Low, Marston, Searle & Rivington, 1886), chapters 12–15.

7. Alfred K. Homma, "O Maranhão Está Chegando," *Correio Agropecuario* 9 (São Paulo: August 1969): 6.

8. Materials on the early stages of this great project are given in Smith, *Brazil* (1972), pp. 647–50.

9. Curiously enough, the way in which this highly commercialized form of monoculture, with its rigid regimentation of a large servile labor force, the very antithesis of the old European feudal system, was generated and spread seems never to have been described in specific terms, but that is a subject for another essay.

10. *The Mechanization of Agriculture in Brazil: A Sociological Study of Minas Gerais* (Gainesville: University of Florida Press, 1969), p. 49. See also pp. 62, 74, and 80 for supplementary statements of the same induction.

11. My first systematic presentation of this schema is in *The Sociology of Rural Life,* 3rd edition (New York: Harper & Brothers, 1953), chapter 14; and subsequent applications of it are found in *Brazil,* 3rd edition, chapter 15; idem, *Colombia: Social Structure and the Process of Development* (Gainesville: University of Florida Press, 1967), chapter 5; and idem, *The Sociology of Agricultural Development* (Leiden: E. J. Brill, 1972), chapter 4.

12. Cf. ibid., *Brazil,* 4th edition, pp. 357–58.

13. Washington, D.C.: The Brazilian Embassy, 1959, p. 1.

14. Cf. T. Lynn Smith, "Agricultural-Pastoral Conflict: A Major Obstacle in the Process of Rural Development," *Journal of Inter-American Studies* 11, no. 1 (January 1969): 16, passim;

idem, "Problems of Agriculture in Latin America," in Committee on Foreign Relations, *Survey of the Alliance for Progress,* Senate Document No. 91-17, 91st Cong., 1st sess. (Washington, D.C.: U.S. Government Printing Office, 1969), pp. 255-56, passim; and idem, "Some Sociocultural Systems Obstructing the Modernization of Agriculture in Spanish America," *Revue Internationale de Sociologie* 7, series 2, no. 1 (1971): 1-10.

Chapter 3

1. Cf. T. Lynn Smith, *Brazil: People and Institutions,* 4th edition (Baton Rouge: Louisiana State University Press, 1972), pp. 631-80; T. Lynn Smith, "The Race between Population and the Food Supply in One Half-Continent: The Case of Brazil," *International Review of Modern Sociology* 2, no. 1 (March 1972): 1-10; and T. Lynn Smith, "Plenty of People Strive To Become a People of Plenty: Salient Features of the Race between Population and the Food Supply in Brazil in the 1970's" (Paper delivered at the III World Congress on Rural Sociology, Baton Rouge, Louisiana, August 22-27, 1972).

2. For maps showing the changes in numbers of inhabitants in Colombia between 1918 and 1938 on a countylike *município* basis and a few comments about the same, see T. Lynn Smith, Justo Diaz Rodriguez, and Luis Roberto Garcia, *Tabio: Estudio de la Organización Social Rural* (Bogotá: Ministerio de la Economia Nacional, 1944), pp. 103-5.

3. Baton Rouge: Louisiana State University Press, 1946.

4. *The Balance of Births and Deaths,* vol. 1 (New York: The Macmillan Company, 1928).

5. New York: The Century Company, 1927.

6. New York: Charles Scribner's Sons, 1928.

7. Washington, D.C.: U.S. Government Printing Office, 1937.

8. For one of the early discussions of the reversal of this trend, see T. Lynn Smith, *Population Analysis* (New York: McGraw-Hill Book Company, 1948), chapter 12.

9. Durham, N.C.: Duke University Press, 1938.

10. Warren S. Thompson and some others, however, remained considerably concerned with population trends in some of the more densely populated parts of the world. See Thompson, *Danger Spots in World Population* (New York: Alfred A. Knopf, Inc., 1929).

11. Cf. his "Esplendor y Decadencia de la Raza Blanca," *Revista de Economía Argentina* 39 (January 1940).

12. New York: McGraw-Hill Book Company, 1948.

13. Eventually this was published as "Tendencias Actuais de População na America Latina," *Sociologia,* vol. 13 (São Paulo: 1951), pp. 135-47.

14. Ibid., pp. 136-38.

15. For data on the trends between 1938 and 1951, see T. Lynn Smith, *Latin American Population Studies* (Gainesville: University of Florida Press, 1960), chapter 5; for those from 1951 to 1964, see T. Lynn Smith, *Studies of Latin American Societies* (New York: Doubleday & Company, 1970), chapter 4.

16. Cf. Inter-American Statistical Institute, "Situación Demográfica: Estado y Movimiento de la Población," *América en Cifras, 1970* (Washington, D.C.: Organization of American States, 1970), p. 96.

17. Inter-American Statistical Institute, *Statistical Compendium of the Americas: 1970* (Washington, D.C.: Organization of American States, 1971), pp. 9-10.

18. T. Lynn Smith, "How High Is the Birth Rate in Colombia?" (Papers of the General Conference, International Union for the Scientific Study of Population, London, 1969), S. 2.4, p. 4.

19. Inter-American Statistical Institute, "Situación Demográfica," *América en Cifras: 1970,* p. 136.

20. The materials from it used here are given in the excellent report by Antonio J. Posada F. and Jeanne de Posada, *The CVT: Challenge to Underdevelopment and Traditionalism* (Bogotá: Ediciones Tercer Mundo, 1966), pp. 46–47.

21. Ibid., p. 47.

22. Especially "Situación Econômica: 1. Agricultura, Ganaderia, Silvicultura, Caza y Pesca," *América en Cifras: 1970* (Washington, D.C.: Organization of American States, 1970), pp. 37–38.

23. Indeed, if one puts any reliance upon the recent attacks in the daily press by conservative journalists, he would conclude that the situation has worsened substantially since 1966, a period that includes the years covered by Colombia's recent four-year plan of agricultural development. See for example the editorials of Camilo Molina Ossa in the *Occidente* of Cali for the years 1970 and 1971 as assembled in his *La Reforma Agraria Colombiana* (Cali: privately printed, 1971). In translation the opening paragraph of Molina's foreword to this volume is as follows:

"Importation of corn, wheat, beans, cocoa, eggs, and milk, and the suspension of exports of meat; the drying up of production in once prosperous zones dedicated to the production of bananas and the ruin of the coconut palms, source of the food supply of the inhabitants of the South Pacific coast of Colombia, to the extent of 300 millions of pesos by the 'Rinchophorus palmarum' bespeak the failure of Agrarian Reform in Colombia. While the nation has the credits, it will combat the hunger. And then? The horrors of the revolt!"

24. For materials about the recent phenomenal increases in Brazil's food supply, see T. Lynn Smith, *Brazil: People and Institutions,* 4th edition (Baton Rouge: Louisiana State University Press, 1972), chapter 24, and chapter 2 of this volume.

25. The list of these is as follows: (1) the size of holdings and what in the Americas is practically synonomous, the size of farms, of which some of the principal types are the highly institutionalized and integrated entities often designated as the "hacienda system," the "plantation system," the "system of family-sized farms," etc.; (2) the land tenure system, involving the kinds of rights those whose livelihoods are dependent upon agricultural and pastoral activities have to the land they use; (3) the system of land surveys and titles; (4) the ways of farming, or the highly standardized and value-laden procedures through which farmers and herdsmen go about the work of getting products from the soil; (5) the type of farming; (6) the family, kinship, domestic, or household system; (7) the educational system; (8) the magico-religious system; (9) the political, administrative, and governmental system; (10) the system of locality groupings, or the neighborhoods and communities into which all societies are differentiated; (11) the system of social stratification, often designated as the class system; (12) the system of communication and transportation; (13) the agricultural credit system; and (14) the marketing system. For the results of my personal endeavors to determine, analyze, and portray the nature and roles of all these sociocultural systems except 5, 12, 13, and 14 in Colombia, Brazil, and other parts of Latin America, see Smith, *Brazil*; T. Lynn Smith, *Colombia: Social Structure and the Process of Development* (Gainesville: University of Florida Press, 1967); and T. Lynn Smith, *The Process of Rural Development in Latin America* (Gainesville: University of Florida Press, 1967). For an even more general discussion of about half of them, see T. Lynn Smith, *The Sociology of Agricultural Development* (Leiden, The Netherlands: E. J. Brill, 1972).

26. Posada and Posada indicate, with reference to this variety of ecological succession in Colombia's Cauca Valley for example, that "small scale crop farming carried on originally by the Indians was moved up into the less fertile lands in the foothills and mountainsides." *The CVT,* p. 50.

27. Translated from *Peregrinación de Alpha* (Bogotá: Arboleda y Valencia, 1914), pp. 12 –13.

28. Ibid., p. 276.

29. The materials on ways of farming in Colombia are drawn mainly from Smith, *Colombia,* chapter 5.

30. Cf. Smith, *Brazil*, pp. 664–75.

31. If one seeks for an explanation of the lag in the development of dairying in the highlands of Colombia, and in equally propitious areas in Venezuela, Ecuador, Peru, and Central America, he must take account of the economy of Spain at the time of the conquest. Following the "cultural shocks" I personally received in 1943 when I began my visits to small farms and haciendas, and now and then a plantation, in all parts of Colombia, I delved into a study of the origins and dissemination of dairy farming as a sociocultural system. My studies soon led me to the knowledge that real dairy husbandry was an achievement of the peoples of north-western Europe and that only the people with cultures that had been transplanted from the countries in that area would know very much about the production of milk and milk products. I then came to see that the dependence of nomadic pastoral peoples, such as those of the steppes of Russia, the Middle East, or North Africa, upon milk and milk products is no critical exception to that rule. The ways in which nomadic peoples get and use milk and cheese never have been and never can be the source of supply for immense populations of great cities. In order to demonstrate clearly the insignificant role of dairying in the entire history of the peoples of the Iberian Peninsula, one should examine Gabriel Alonso de Herrera's classic work entitled *Agricultura General.* First published in Madrid in 1513, this monumental treatise was repub-lished time after time, with additions supplied by various generations of editors. In the edition of 1818 put out under the auspices of the Real Sociedad Económica de Madrid, the original with all the additions runs to 2,026 pages in four very large volumes. In all these pages, however, less than one is devoted to milk cows and milk products, and most of the comment found there concerns some cows from the Netherlands and Switzerland that the most recent editors had seen in Madrid.

32. Cf. T. Lynn Smith, "Colonization and Settlement in Colombia," *Rural Sociology* 12, no. 2 (June 1947): 132, and T. Lynn Smith, "Agricultural-Pastoral Conflict: A Major Obstacle in the Process of Rural Development," *Journal of Inter-American Affairs* 10, no. 1 (January 1969): 16–43, for indications of early and sustained concern about these matters and efforts to effect changes.

Chapter 4

1. See T. Lynn Smith, "Migration from One Latin American Country to Another," in *International Population Conference,* edited by Louis Henry and Wilhelm Winkler (Vienna: Im Selbstverlag, 1959), pp. 695–700.

2. See T. Lynn Smith, "How High Is the Birth Rate in Colombia?" (Papers presented to the Conference of the International Union for the Scientific Study of Population, London, 1969). In Colombian reports to the Organization of American States, the United Nations, and so on, the data on baptisms by the Roman Catholic church are given as the figures on the numbers of births occuring. These are the materials for Colombia carried regularly in the great compendiums of demographic data such as *The Demographic Yearbook* of the United Nations and *América en Cifras* issued by the Organization of American States. On this basis the figures on the crude birth rates in Colombia generally fluctuate around 35 per 1000 population, although sometimes they are considerably lower. The final conclusion of the study cited here, in the course of which various other materials were used including the analysis of the ratio of children under five to women aged fifteen to forty-four, is as follows: "The analyses presented in this paper supply the basis for concluding that the birth rate in Colombia is at least 45, that it probably is about 47 or 48, and that it may be as high as 50 per 1000 population."

3. See T. Lynn Smith, *Latin American Population Studies,* University of Florida Social Science Monographs no. 8 (Gainesville: University of Florida Press, 1960), p. 71.

Chapter 5

1. See for example T. Lynn Smith, *Brazil: People and Institutions,* 4th edition (Baton Rouge: Louisiana State University Press, 1972), pp. 148–50; and T. Lynn Smith, *Latin American Population Studies* (Gainesville: University of Florida Press, 1960), pp. 56–59.

2. For some of the general information about the rapid growth of the "suburbs," see T. Lynn Smith, "Los Problemas Sociales de la Actualidad on la America Latina," in *Memoria, VI Congreso Latino-americano de Sociología,* Tomo II (Caracas: Imprenta Nacional, 1961), pp. 419–23; and for a detailed study of the haphazard way of life characteristic of them, see Manuel Zabala C., *Estudio Social sobre un Barrio de Invasión* (Cali: Facultad de Arquitectura, Universidad del Valle, 1964). For one of the more ambitious projects for planning and putting into effect the measures needed to correct the situation, at least in part, see Gobierno de Peru, *Ley de Remodelación, Saneamiento y Legalización de los Barrios Marginales* (Lima: Senado de la República, 1961). See also Smith, *Brazil,* chapters 22 and 25.

3. T. Lynn Smith, "Studies of Colonization and Settlement," *Latin American Research Review* 4, no. 1 (Winter 1969): 109.

Chapter 6

1. Anyone desiring to have information about some of the qualitative aspects is referred to my previous publications and especially to *Brazil: People and Institutions,* 4th edition (Baton Rouge: Louisiana State University, 1972) and *Studies of Latin American Societies* (New York: Doubleday & Company, 1970).

2. Cf. T. Lynn Smith, "Migration from One Latin American Country to Another," in *International Population Conference (Congrés International de la Population),* edited by Louis Henry and Wilhelm Winkler (Vienna: Im Selbstverlag, 1959), pp. 695–700.

3. For some of the preliminary results of a comprehensive study of Cuban escapees, that is, those who have used hazardous means to flee the island, see Juan L. Clark, "The Cuban Escapees," *Latinamericanist* 6, University of Florida (November 1970).

4. T. Lynn Smith, *Brazil: People and Institutions,* 1st edition (Baton Rouge: Louisiana State University Press, 1946), pp. 160–64, passim.

Chapter 7

1. These are as follows:

a. *Agrarian Reform in Latin America* (New York: Alfred A. Knopf, Inc., 1965).

b. *Brazil: People and Institutions,* 3rd edition (Baton Rouge: Louisiana State University Press, 1963), chapters 9, 10, 12, 13, 14, and 15.

c. *Colombia: Social Structure and the Process of Development* (Gainesville: University of Florida Press, 1967).

d. *Current Social Trends and Problems in Latin America,* Latin American Monographs no. 1 (Gainesville: University of Florida Press, 1957).

e. "The Growth of Population in Central and South America," in *Study of Population and Immigration Problems: Western Hemisphere* (II), U.S. House of Representatives, Committee on the Judiciary (Washington, D.C.: Government Printing Office, 1963), pp. 125–84.

f. "Hunger and Antiquated Farming in Latin America," *The Catholic World* 205, no. 1,229 (August 1967): 268–75.

g. *The Process of Rural Development in Latin America,* University of Florida Social Science Monographs no. 33 (Gainesville: University of Florida Press, 1967).

2. *INCORA, 1964: Third Year of Agrarian Reform in Colombia* (Bogotá: Imprensa Nacional de Colombia, 1965), p. 3.

3. "Brazil: Complex Giant," *Foreign Affairs* (January 1965): 303–4.

4. Thomas Nixon Carver, *Principles of Rural Economics* (Boston: Ginn and Company, 1911), p. 104.

5. Charles Wayland Towne and Edward Norris Wentworth, *Pigs: From Cave to Corn Belt* (Norman: University of Oklahoma Press, 1950), p. 11.

6. Ibid., p. 211.

Chapter 8

1. Richard F. Burton, *The Highlands of the Brazil,* vol. 1 (London: Tinsley Brothers, 1868), p. 47.

2. T. Lynn Smith, *Brazil: People and Institutions* (Baton Rouge: Louisiana State University Press, 1946), p. 483.

3. F. J. Oliveira Vianna, "O Povo Brazileiro e Sua Evolção," *Recenseamento do Brazil, 1920,* vol. 1 (Rio de Janeiro: Imprenta Nacional, 1922), p. 282.

4. Edward A. Ross, *South of Panama* (New York: The Century Company, 1915), p. 144. The italics are in the original.

5. Translated from Gilberto Freyre, "La lucha no es de clases," *Life en Español* (May 11, 1964): 25–26.

Chapter 9

1. Carl C. Taylor, *Rural Life in Argentina* (Baton Rouge: Louisiana State University Press, 1948), p. 219.

2. For many additional interesting details see William Frederic Badè, *The Old Testament in the Light of Today: A Study in Moral Development* (Boston and New York: Houghton Mifflin Company, 1915), passim.

3. Cf. Don Martindale, *The Nature and Types of Sociological Theory* (Boston: Houghton Mifflin Company, 1960), p. 309.

4. Gustave Le Bon, *La civilización de los Arabes,* trans. Luis Carreras (Barcelona: Montaner y Simon, 1886), pp. 181–82.

5. Hugh Foot, *A Start in Freedom* (London: Hodder and Stoughton, 1964), pp. 145–46.

6. Joseph Townsend, *A Journey through Spain in the Years 1786 and 1787 . . . ,* vol. 2 (London: C. Dilly, 1791), pp. 61–63, 64, 227, and 284–85.

7. *Informe de la Sociedad Económica de Madrid al Real y Supremo Consejo de Castilla en el Expediente de Ley Agraria,* nueva edición (Madrid: Imprenta de I. Sancha, 1820), p. 77. For a lengthy study of the Mesta see Julius Klein, *The Mesta* (Cambridge: Harvard University Press, 1920).

8. Cf. William H. Dusenberry, *The Mexican Mesta* (Urbana: University of Illinois Press, 1963), passim.

9. An analysis and description of the transformation of Spain from a country of agriculturists to one dominated by sheep and cattle interests is given in T. Lynn Smith, "Some Neglected Spanish Social Thinkers," *The Americas* 27, no. 1 (July 1960): 37–52; see also Smith, *Colombia,* pp. 189–95

10. Manuel Ancizar, *Peregrinación de Alpha* (Bogotá: Arboleda y Valencia, 1914), pp. 12–13. See Chapter 3, pages 39–40, for further remarks by Ancizar.

11. For further information about agrarian reform in many of the countries, see T. Lynn Smith, ed., *Agrarian Reform in Latin America* (New York: Alfred A. Knopf, Inc., 1965). There are some exceptions to the rule that agrarian reform endeavors in Latin America are part and parcel of the conflict between pastoral and agricultural interests. In Cuba and El Salvador, specifically, the unfulfilled hopes of the peasants to acquire the ownership of the land necessarily had to be directed toward the subdivision of the great sugar-cane plantations and large coffee plantations, respectively.

12. Frank L. Owsley, *Plain Folks of the Old South* (Baton Rouge: Louisiana State University Press, 1949), p. 34.

13. Ibid., p. 51.

14. Edward I. Moe and Carl C. Taylor, *Culture of a Contemporary Community: Irwin, Iowa,* Rural Life Studies, no. 5 (Washington, D.C.: U.S. Department of Agriculture, 1942), pp. 5–6.

15. Ibid., p. 20.

16. Some very readable observations about this are to be found in E. C. Branson, *Farm Life Abroad* (Chapel Hill: University of North Carolina Press, 1924), pp. 84–255; and H. Rider Haggard, *Rural Denmark and Its Lessons* (London: Longmans, Green and Co., 1917).

17. The term satisfactory is used deliberately. I maintain that the corn–hog–beef-cattle type of farming characteristic of the midwestern part of the United States is the most satisfactory because: (1) through it farmers attain the greatest average production per man-year that has been achieved; (2) the fact that the system is one involving middle-class operators of family-sized farms almost exclusively, so that families headed by farm laborers are conspicuous by their absence, secures a highly equitable distribution of the benefits of the production among all those who have a share in the productive process; (3) as a result of this, and also because of the inclusion within the system of production for home use of substantial amounts of dairy, poultry, garden, and fruit products, the average level of living of the families involved reaches the maximum ever achieved by an agricultural population; (4) all of this contributes heavily to a high type of community life; and (5) the individuals born and reared within the system taken as a whole come nearer to attaining the potentials of the human personality than is true of any other large agricultural population.

18. Thomas Nixon Carver, *Principles of Rural Economics* (Boston: Ginn and Company, 1911), p. 104 (italics are mine). The last two sentences of this paragraph are used almost verbatim by Walter W. Jennings in his *History of Economic Progress in the United States* (New York: Thomas Y. Crowell Company, 1926), p. 399.

19. Carl C. Taylor and Associates, *Rural Life in the United States* (New York: Alfred A. Knopf, Inc., 1949), pp. 366–67.

20. New York: The Macmillan Company, 1947.

21. Ibid., pp. 285–87.

22. Norman: University of Oklahoma Press, 1950.

23. Ibid., facing p. 10.

24. Ibid., pp. 210–11.

25. Cf. Samuel Deane, *The New England Farmer* (Boston: Wells and Lilly, 1822), p. 447; and *The Farmers' Cabinet; Devoted to Agriculture, Horticulture, and Rural Economy,* vol. 2 (Philadelphia, 1838), p. 268.

26. See the *Report of the Commissioner of Patents, for the Year 1849,* part 2, "Agriculture" (Washington: Office of Printers to the Senate, 1850), pp. 87, 101, 102, 105, 112, 148, 151, 185, 225, 227, 228, and 240–41.

27. See John Filson's "Map of Kentucke" drawn in 1784 and dedicated to George Washington, which was reproduced in Willard Rouse Jillson, *The Kentucky Country* (Washington: H. L. and J. B. McQueen, 1931). On this the designations of "Fine Cane," "Fine Cane Land,"

and "Abundance of Cane" are by far the most prominent indications of the resources of the territory.

28. *Plain Folks of the Old South,* pp. 63–64.

29. This important contribution appeared in the *Ohio Archaeological and Historical Publications* vol. 22 (Columbus: Published for the Society, 1913), p. 188. I am indebted to Mr. Charleton Myers of Morral, Ohio, for directing me to this source.

30. *Report of the Commissioner,* pp. 298–99. See also E. W. Sheets, O. E. Baker, C. E. Gibbons, O. C. Stine, and R. H. Wilcox, "Our Beef Supply," in *United States Department of Agriculture Yearbook 1921* (Washington: Government Printing Office, 1922), p. 233.

31. *The Farmers' Cabinet,* vol. 1, pp. 154–55.

32. See the excellent discussion of the importations of cattle of various types by Charles L. Flint, "Progress in Agriculture," in *One Hundred Years' Progress of the United States* (Hartford, Conn.: L. Stebbins, 1870), especially pp. 47–48.

33. If the reader will keep in mind the types of hogs then prevailing on the frontier, and even running wild in large numbers in the woods and on the prairies in Ohio, Kentucky, and the states and territories to the west of them, it will not seem so strange that tens of thousands of *big* "pigs went to market" under their own power. The swine brought to what is now the United States by DeSoto, those imported by the settlers at Jamestown, and those introduced into New England were all of the *Sus scrofa* group, whose general characteristics were those of the wild boar from which they descended. Only later did crosses with varieties of the *Sus indicus* (the lard type of hog from southeastern Asia) such as the Berkshires (from England) and the Poland China (developed in Ohio itself) come to be of importance. For the essential facts about the two great groups of swine that were crossed to develop the highly efficient modern breeds, see Charles Darwin, *The Variation of Plants and Animals under Domestication,* vol. 1 (New York: D. Appleton and Company, 1899), pp. 66–80. *One Hundred Years' Progress,* p. 64, has given us the following description of the types of hogs then prevailing in the United States:

"Previous to the introduction of the Woburn hog ['a fortunate cross of the Chinese and the large English hog' brought to the United States near the close of the eighteenth century], the classes of swine that had prevailed in the eastern and middle states were coarse, long-legged, large-boned, slab-sided, and flab-eared, an unprofitable and unsightly beast, better calculated for subsoiling than for filling a pork barrel. . . . The native hogs of the west—that is, the descendants of those taken there by earlier settlers, and common there till within a very recent period—were admirably calculated for the primitive condition of civilization in which they were placed. They were well calculated to shirk [*sic*] for themselves, as they had to do, and became fleet as the deer, while their strength of head, neck, and tusks enabled them to fight any wild beast of the forest, and withstand any extent of exposure to the weather."

And Frederick Law Olmstead, whose descriptions of life and labor in the area to the south of the Ohio River on the eve of the Civil War are unrivaled, has given us the following word picture of these swine in action: "Of living creatures, for miles, not one was to be seen . . . except hogs. These—long, lank, bony, snake-headed, hairy wild beasts—would come dashing across our path, in packs of from three to a dozen, with short, hasty grunts, almost always at a gallop, and looking neither to right nor left, as if they were in pursuit of a fox, and were quite certain to catch him in the next hundred yards." *Journey in the Seaboard Slave States, with Remarks on Their Economy* (New York: Dix and Edwards, 1856), pp. 65–66.

34. R. Carlyle Buley, *The Old Northwest,* vol. 1 (Bloomington: Indiana University Press, 1951), p. 480.

35. New York: C. M. Saxton.

36. Ibid., pp. 265–67.

37. Consider in this connection the comments of one visitor who appraised the potentials of Illinois with the eye of an experienced farmer in 1834:

"Peoria is about the geographical centre of Illinois, though by no means as yet the centre of population, which is still far to the south-east. . . . The adjacent country is very fertile. *The soil, like that of Illinois generally, is better suited to the grazier than the agriculturist.* It is composed of a black and rich mould, with a small admixture of fine silicious sand, and rests on soft permeable clay without being interspersed with stone or gravel. This information, while it is unfavourable to the existence of perennial streams and fountains, and impedes the plough of the agriculturist, and endangers his health by the creation of miasma, yet in the vicinity of the middle lands furnishes inexhaustible meadows to the grazier, and every facility for canals and railroads." C. F. Hoffman, *A Winter in the Far West,* vol. 2 (London: Richard Bentley, 1835), p. 58 (italics added).

As a sidelight it seems worth mentioning that at almost exactly the time of Hoffman's visit to this section of Illinois, in the same general area Abraham Lincoln, while tending store, in the hours when trade was slack established his reputation as a rail splitter by cutting enough rails to make a pen for one thousand hogs. Carl Sandburg, *Abraham Lincoln: The Prairie Years,* vol. 1 (New York: Harcourt, Brace, and Company, 1926), p. 138. Sandburg also mentions the wild hogs that ranged over the prairies in 1830 when Lincoln moved from Indiana to Illinois. Ibid., pp. 106, 133.

38. Cf. Smith, *The Process of Rural Development in Latin America,* pp. 38–39.

39. Cf. Pedro de Aguado, *Primera Parte de la Recopilación Historial Resolutoria de Sancta Marta y Nuevo Reino de Granada de las Indias del Mar Océano,* Tomo I (Madrid: Espasa-Calpe, S. A., 1930), pp. 250, 253.

40. Inter-American Committee on Agricultural Development, *Ecuador: Study of Agricultural Education, Investigation and Extension, 1965* (Washington: Pan American Union [1968?]), pp. 8–11.

41. Cf. Joseph Cannon Bailey, *Seaman A. Knapp* (New York: Columbia University Press, 1945), pp. 55–63, 110–23, passim.

Chapter 10

1. Inter-American Statistical Institute, "Situación Económica: . . .," *América en Cifras, 1970* (Washington, D.C.: Organization of American States, 1970), p. 155.

2. Ibid., p. 151; and *Anuário Estatístico do Brasil, 1962* (Rio de Janeiro: Instituto Brasileiro de Geografia e Estatística, 1962), p. 57.

3. Alfredo K. Homma,, "O Maranhão Está Chegando," *Correio Agropecuario* 9 (August 1969): 6. In a report on *Transamazonian Highways* (Montreal, Canada, 1970), p. 22, which Brazil's Ministry of Transportation presented to the VI World Meeting of the International Road Federation, the following changes between 1960 and 1970 in the area traversed by the Belém-Brasília Highway are indicated: population, an increase from 100,000 to 2,000,000 inhabitants; number of cities and villages, an increase from 10 to 120; number of cattle, from negligible to 5,000,000 head; farming, from a little subsistence agriculture to intensive cultures of corn, beans, rice, and cotton.

4. Translated from the announcement in the March 18, 1970, issue of the *Boletim Especial* distributed by the Brazilian Embassy, Washington, D.C.

5. Ibid., October 12, 1970.

6. Ibid., January 12, 1971.

7. The fullest account of these that I have been able to obtain is given in *Extensão Rural,* a monthly published by the Associação Brasileira de Crédito e Assistência Rural—ABCAR, Rio de Janeiro, vol. 5 (Agosto 1970):8–13. The materials in the paragraphs that follow were taken from it.

8. Alfred Russell Wallace, *Travels on the Amazon* (London: Ward, Lock & Co., 1911), pp. 230–32.

9. Cf. Herbert H. Smith, *Brazil: The Amazons and the Coast* (New York: Charles Scribner's Sons, 1879), pp. 135–76.

Chapter 11

1. See Chapter 3, note 31.

2. See pp. 57, 67, 70, 73, 84, 93–94, 97, and 99 of the second edition of T. Lynn Smith, *Brazil: People and Institutions* (Baton Rouge: Louisiana State University Press, 1954).

3. Gilberto Freyre, *The Masters and the Slaves: A Study in the Development of Brazilian Civilization,* trans. Samuel Putman (New York: Alfred A. Knopf, Inc., 1946), p. 52. This is one of the two references to milk in the entire volume. The other on p. 46 merely mentions the lack of milk in a list of dietary deficiencies. In the preface to the English edition, p. xlix, he gives "as a result of monoculture, an irregularity and deficiency in the supply of foodstuffs such as meat, milk, eggs, and vegetables."

4. A metric ton is equal to 2,204.6 pounds or 1,000 liters.

5. *Anuário Estatístico do Brasil, 1952,* vol. 13 (Rio de Janeiro: Instituto Brasileiro de Geografia e Estatística, 1953), p. 202. It should be indicated that the bulk of the pasteurized milk produced in the state of Rio de Janeiro is consumed in Guanabara, and most of that produced in Minas Gerais goes to the cities of São Paulo and Rio de Janeiro.

6. The data for 1960 are taken from the *Anuário Estatístico do Brasil, 1962,* vol. 23 (Rio de Janeiro: Instituto Brasileiro de Geografia e Estatística, 1963), pp. 66, 102.

7. See John McDonald, "Brazil's Expanding Production and Trade," *Foreign Agriculture* 7 (August 25, 1969): 7–9.

8. Carlos Borges Schmidt, "Rural Life in Brazil," in T. Lynn Smith and Alexander Marchant, eds., *Brazil: Portrait of Half a Continent* (New York: The Dryden Press, 1951), pp. 185–86.

9. Ibid., pp. 186–87.

10. For many of the details of the social organization and way of life of the people of the Paraitinga Valley as they were at about the time Schmidt called attention to the transformation that was under way, see J. V. Freitas Marcondes and T. Lynn Smith, "The Caipira of the Paraitinga Valley, Brazil," *Social Forces* 31 (October 1952):47–53.

11. The name comes from the three countries sponsoring and financing the projects, namely Holland, America (the United States), and Brazil. For some of the more significant facts about the history and operations of these dairymen, see C. S. J. Hogenboom, "Plano de Investimento da Holambra," and "O Projeto da Holambra II," in José Arthur Rios, *Recomendaçoes sôbre Reforma Agrária* (Rio de Janeiro: Instituto Brasileiro de Ação Democrática, 1961), pp. 301–27.

12. Submitted to the graduate school, University of Florida, December 1966. Subsequently, a part of this study, which omitted, however, the lengthy chapter of quotations from his daily journal referred to here, was published under the title *The Mechanization of Agriculture in Brazil* (Gainesville: University of Florida Press, 1969).

13. Clements, "A Sociological Study of the Mechanization of Agriculture in Minas Gerais, Brazil" (Ph.D. dissertation, University of Florida, 1966), pp. 26–27.

14. Ibid., p. 35.

15. Ibid., p. 36.

16. Ibid., p. 37.

17. Ibid., pp. 39–40.

18. Ibid., p. 42.

19. See Minnich, "A Sociological Study of the Mennonite Immigrant Communities in Paraná, Brazil," submitted to the graduate school, University of Florida, June 1966, pp. 117–212.

20. These data are from Altiva Pilatti Balhana, Brasil Pinheiro Machado et al., *Campos Gerais: Estruturas Agrárias* (Curitiba, 1968), pp. 89, 93, 114.

21. *Survey of the Brazilian Economy for 1966* (Washington, D.C.: The Brazilian Embassy, 1967), p. 95, states that "in some areas of Brazil, it is difficult to establish a clear distinction between beef and dairy cattle; many farmers, as a result of poor milk production, use the same cattle for both purposes. On the other hand, there are no statistics for the numbers of the different breeds of cattle raised in the country as a whole."

22. Some of the highlights of the announced "Metas e Bases para a Ação de Govêrno," including the measures designed to promote dairy husbandry and to enlarge and modernize milk-processing plants, are given in "Acão Programada para o Ingreso no Mundo Desenvolvido," *Extensão Rural* 5, no. 58 (Outubro 1970): 3–13.

Chapter 12

1. *Compton's Pictured Encyclopedia and Fact-Index,* vol. 1 (Chicago, 1944), p. 47.

2. Alfred Russell Wallace, *Travels on the Amazon* (London: Ward, Lock & Company, 1911), p. 177.

3. Ibid., pp. 230–31.

4. Interestingly enough, however, this way of farming was used for many years in the production of rice in southwestern Louisiana. There on the extensive prairies, here and there on the almost perfectly level land, the old buffalo wallows came to be large ponds dotted about the water-logged area. There the French-Acadian settlers carried on a rudimentary pastoral culture similar in most essential respects to the cattle ranching still prevailing widely throughout much of Latin America. These Acadians hit upon the device of broadcasting rice grains in the areas immediately above the water lines of the ponds, and then riding their ponies over the ground to sink the seeds into the mud. If the ensuing summer was a wet one, they got modest harvests, and if it was dry they had nothing to show for their efforts—the crop depended entirely upon Providence. Hence, the grain was called "providence rice" and was produced in this way in the area until 1883, when farmers from Iowa and Illinois who had been attracted to the area discovered they could use the system of wheat culture recently perfected in the Midwest to grow rice on the Louisiana prairies. All modern rice culture stems from this important discovery, including the production of rice in many of the Latin American countries.

5. This translation appears in T. Lynn Smith, *Colombia: Social Structure and the Process of Development* (Gainesville: University of Florida Press, 1967), p. 201. The lines translated are from Medardo Rivas, *Los Trabajadores de Tierra Caliente* (Bogotá: Imprenta y Librería M. Rivas, 1899), p. 58.

6. See Smith, *Colombia,* pp. 221–23; T. Lynn Smith, *Studies of Latin American Societies* (New York: Doubleday & Company, 1970), pp. 271–72; and Orlando Fals Borda, *Facts and Theory of Sociocultural Change in a Rural Social System,* Monografías Sociológicas No. 2 (Bogotá: Universidad National de Colombia, 1960), pp. 19–20.

7. *Men, Machines, and the Land* (Chicago: Farm and Industrial Equipment Institute, 1974), pp. 19–21.

Author Index

Subject Index

absentee ownership, 40, 105
advanced plow culture, 18, 19–20, 44, 160, 171–73, 175
African slaves, 9
agrarian reform, 40, 93, 98–99, 113, 115, 140, 181, 185
agricultural vs. pastoral activities, 16–17, 91–92, 106–31
agriculture: mechanization of, 17, 19–20, 45, 90–91, 129, 173–76, 177; origins of, 161–62; problems of, 89–96
alfalfa, 23, 121, 139

Belém-Brasília Highway, 14–16, 76, 136, 140
birth control, 84–85
birth rate, 4, 30, 31–32, 33–34, 35, 47, 58–60, 61, 68, 84–85, 176, 182

campesinos, 40, 43, 131
cattle ranching, 16–17, 41, 115, 118–19
Census of the Americas, 29, 52–53
cattlemen vs. "sodbusters," 115–18, 130
cities, growth of, 71–76, 119–20, 153
class system, 101, 102–105, 181
colonization, 135–41
colonos, 40, 144
community, metropolitan, 37
comparative method, 3–4
corn, 23, 95–96, 106, 123–25, 131–32
corn-hog-beef cattle type of farming, 47, 95–96, 106–107, 117, 118–30, 132, 185

dairying, 22–23, 46–47, 107, 118–19, 142–54, 182
death rate, 11–12, 30, 31, 34, 35, 59, 60, 61, 79, 177
"declining population," 27
demographic revolution, 28–29
demographic sophisms, 65–68
demographic transition, 11, 33
depopulation 90–91
digging stick, 158, 167
Dutch immigrants, 148, 156

economic functions, 122
egress, freedom of, 80, 82–83
emigration, 56–68, 81–82

factors of production, 40
falta de braços, 19, 85
family planning, 84–85
family-sized farms, 41, 44, 100–101, 122, 129, 185
felling and burning, 18, 19, 42–43, 136, 160, 165–67, 177
"fire agriculture," *see* felling and burning
food production, obstacles to increased, 87–132
food supply, 12–24, 35–38, 41, 42, 46–47, 135, 158, 176–77, 181
goats, 109–10

hacienda system, 38–41, 113, 115, 181
highways, 14–16, 76, 77, 116, 136–41, 187

193